T0026804

ELECTRIC PRESSURE COOKER
CURRY COOKBOOK

ELECTRIC PRESSURE COOKER

CURRY COOKBOOK

75 RECIPES FROM INDIA, THAILAND, THE CARIBBEAN, AND BEYOND

ANEESHA GUPTA

PHOTOGRAPHY BY ANNIE MARTIN

ROCKRIDGE
PRESS

Copyright © 2020 by Rockridge Press, Emeryville, California

No part of this publication may be reproduced, stored in a retrieval system, or transmitted in any form or by any means, electronic, mechanical, photocopying, recording, scanning, or otherwise, except as permitted under Sections 107 or 108 of the 1976 United States Copyright Act, without the prior written permission of the Publisher. Requests to the Publisher for permission should be addressed to the Permissions Department, Rockridge Press, 6005 Shellmound Street, Suite 175, Emeryville, CA 94608.

Limit of Liability/Disclaimer of Warranty: The Publisher and the author make no representations or warranties with respect to the accuracy or completeness of the contents of this work and specifically disclaim all warranties, including without limitation warranties of fitness for a particular purpose. No warranty may be created or extended by sales or promotional materials. The advice and strategies contained herein may not be suitable for every situation. This work is sold with the understanding that the Publisher is not engaged in rendering medical, legal, or other professional advice or services. If professional assistance is required, the services of a competent professional person should be sought. Neither the Publisher nor the author shall be liable for damages arising herefrom. The fact that an individual, organization, or website is referred to in this work as a citation and/or potential source of further information does not mean that the author or the Publisher endorses the information the individual, organization, or website may provide or recommendations they/it may make. Further, readers should be aware that websites listed in this work may have changed or disappeared between when this work was written and when it is read.

For general information on our other products and services or to obtain technical support, please contact our Customer Care Department within the United States at (866) 744-2665, or outside the United States at (510) 253-0500.

Rockridge Press publishes its books in a variety of electronic and print formats. Some content that appears in print may not be available in electronic books, and vice versa.

TRADEMARKS: Rockridge Press and the Rockridge Press logo are trademarks or registered trademarks of Callisto Media Inc. and/or its affiliates, in the United States and other countries, and may not be used without written permission. All other trademarks are the property of their respective owners. Rockridge Press is not associated with any product or vendor mentioned in this book.

Interior and Cover Designer: Elizabeth Zuhl
Art Producer: Meg Baggott
Editor: Gurvinder Singh Gandu
Photography © 2020 Annie Martin. Food styling by Oscar Molinar
Author photo courtesy of Arushi Gupta & Tanvi Gupta

ISBN: Print 978-1-64739-206-2
eBook 978-1-64739-207-9
R0

TO MY DAD, MY BIGGEST SUPPORTER! I MISS YOU A LOT EVERY SINGLE DAY.

TO MY MOM, FOR TEACHING ME HOW TO COOK SMART, NOT HARD.

TO MY HUSBAND AND DAUGHTERS, MY LIFELINES!

CONTENTS

INTRODUCTION

Hi there. I'm Aneesha, a foodie by birth, who turned a passion for cooking into a recipe blog at SpiceCravings.com. On my blog, I share my family's favorite global recipes that are low in effort and big on taste, thanks to smart cooking appliances like an electric pressure cooker.

I started cooking in my early teens in India by helping my mother in the kitchen and inherited her recipes for traditional North Indian Punjabi food, including many classic curries, like Rajma, Chole, Butter Chicken, and Dal.

I learned from my mother that you don't have to spend hours in the kitchen to make tasty and healthy meals for the family—and the pressure cooker played a big part in that. Mom always used her stovetop pressure cooker for making beans, lentils, and meat curries. So, naturally, I became a pro at pressure cooking very early on.

In my early travel-heavy career as a flight attendant, I was exposed to cuisines from around the world, and then 20 years ago I settled down in California, a melting pot of all cuisines. I was amazed at how every culture and region has their spin on a basic curry. Over the years, I adapted these recipes for my stovetop pressure cooker and achieved the same results with much less time and effort.

About four years ago, I bought my first electric pressure cooker, an Instant Pot, during a Black Friday sale. The level of convenience it added to my life amazed me. Back then, as a graphic designer, my average day was filled with client meetings, deadlines, and kids' after-school activities, and then I had the challenge of cooking a healthy meal for my family in a short amount of time. I felt like the electric pressure cooker was a godsend. I could sauté in it, fill the pot with ingredients, set it to cook, and walk away! No monitoring or heat adjustments needed—that was a game-changer for me.

Electric pressure cookers are ideal for making curry for three reasons. First, they provide a gentle and consistent heat, which allows the spices to release their natural oils and aromas and ingredients to infuse their flavors in each other, so the result mimics the taste of a slow-cooked curry. Second, it's a huge time-saver. I can turn dried beans or tough cuts of meat into that "melt-in-the-mouth" texture in an hour, most of which is hands-off cooking time. Third, cooking a curry in an electric pressure cooker is as simple as sauté, fill, and start. Even my husband and teen girls have become curry experts now.

In 2017, I started Spice Cravings as an online resource for my teenage kids to teach them an essential life skill—cooking—and the electric pressure cooker made that possible. The blog soon became a platform to share easy recipes for busy families like mine. And with this book, I continue that effort.

This book is for all curry lovers—beginners and advanced cooks alike. Whether you're cooking for two or 20, these easy-to-follow directions will help you master the world of curries in your electric pressure cookers. If you have any questions about these recipes, send me a message on my blog, SpiceCravings.com, or my Facebook or Instagram page (facebook. com/spicecravings and instagram.com/spicecravings), and I'll be happy to help. On that note, I hope you enjoy cooking these recipes as much as I've enjoyed developing and testing them. Happy cooking!

Curry: A Saucy History

Who doesn't love a bowl of hot curry soaked up with naan or rice? It's food for the soul!

Did you know that this mystic dish is eaten by more than half the world and has been around since the 15th century?

The origin of curry can be traced to the Indus Valley civilization, dating back to 2600 BCE. Archaeological evidence from Mohenjo-Daro suggests the use of a mortar and pestle to pound spices like cumin, mustard, fennel, and tamarind pods to flavor food.

So, what exactly is curry? Curry means many things in many different regions. Curry is a generic term that refers to a spiced dish originating from the Indian subcontinent or from Southeast Asia. Curry is eaten in many countries, including India, Pakistan, Bangladesh, Nepal, Myanmar, Sri Lanka, Thailand, Malaysia, Indonesia, Jamaica, the United States, and England, to name just a few.

Curry can be wet or dry. Dry curries are cooked with just enough liquid to coat the ingredients in the spice mixture, whereas wet curries often include either a tomato, yogurt, coconut milk, or cream sauce, or gravy. It is usually eaten with rice or a flatbread, like roti or naan.

Curry originated in India thousands of years ago and the word comes from the Tamil (Indian language) word *kari*, which refers to a meat- or vegetable-based stew. In the early 1500s, after the Portuguese captured Goa in India, they introduced chilies to the local stews and called them *carel*. In the 18th century, when the British came to India, they transformed *carel* to *curry*.

Curry powder, which is a popular premixed spice blend, didn't come from India at all but in fact is an 18th-century British invention. It's a blend of coriander, cumin, ginger, black pepper, cardamom, mustard, cayenne, and turmeric, which gives it the yellow color. The first curry powder recipe in Britain appeared in the book *The Art of Cookery Made Plain and Easy,* by Hannah Glasse in 1747.

The British can be given credit for spreading curry across the world. Popular dishes like Coronation Chicken and Jubilee Chicken, in which cooked chicken was served with a curry-flavored creamy sauce, were created in mid-1900s to celebrate different British monarchs, including Queen Elizabeth II.

During the 19th century, colonization, Indian migrations, and international trade further spread curry to other Asian countries, Europe, and South Africa. Curry was even carried to the Caribbean by Indian laborers who worked on the British cane plantations.

As curry traveled, it was adapted and modified to incorporate local ingredients and cooking techniques, which is why there are so many variants around the world.

Every curry dish has a unique taste, color, and heat level depending on the specific spice blend, ingredients, and regional influences. For example, the Mughal Empire (15th century) influenced curries in northern India, so a chicken curry made in the north may taste and look very different than one made in southern India. Similarly, Thai Green Curry tastes quite different from Thai Massaman Curry due to the ingredients used in the curry paste.

While this book is certainly not a comprehensive collection of every existing curry, I am presenting a range of popular world curries, ones you might have enjoyed at local restaurants, and that can be made with easily available ingredients. I hope you enjoy them as much as my family does.

CHAPTER 1

MAKING CURRY IN AN INSTANT

Electric pressure cookers have been an integral part of my kitchen in recent years.

They are a huge time-saver, and I love how ingredients get a chance to blend together in an electric pressure cooker. Whether you're cooking soups, stews, or, in this instance, curry, the result is always a perfect harmony of infused flavors.

Even though stovetop pressure cookers have been used for such a long time, especially in countries like India, they can seem intimidating to many people and do require some careful monitoring.

Fortunately, the current fleet of electric pressure cookers that are so popular today, like the Instant Pot, have bridged the gap between tradition and convenience. These "smart cookers" enable a home cook to program and automate the cooking process without having to babysit the appliance. I can follow the instructions for a recipe, fill the pot, seal and set it for pressure cooking, and *walk away*. I couldn't imagine that level of convenience until a few years ago.

Benefits of Cooking with an Electric Pressure Cooker

Pressure cooking is when food is cooked in a sealed vessel at high pressure with water or other liquid. The higher pressure limits the liquid's ability to boil by trapping steam, which raises the atmospheric pressure inside the pressure cooker. This makes the boiling point of the liquid 250 degrees Fahrenheit instead of the normal 212 degrees, which is how it cooks food faster.

Here are some of the many reasons why an electric pressure cooker is the perfect appliance for making curry:

1. **You save time:** Red meat and bean curries require a long cooking time. Pressure cooking cuts that active cooking time in half. Not only does it save time, but it also reduces energy usage.

2. **It allows hands-off cooking:** This is a huge advantage, especially for curries that take a long time to cook. Once you initiate the pressure cooking process, the cooker takes care of all the work from there. You don't have to monitor it or make any heat adjustments.

3. **You can multitask:** Using the pot-in-pot cooking style, you can make the whole meal in your cooker at the same time, like rice with chicken curry. With simple accessories, you can cook multiple items simultaneously.

4. **The controls are simple and straightforward:** With built-in presets like "beans," "rice," and "meat," all you have to do is push a few buttons and follow the steps and the recipes come out consistent every time.

5. **It locks in nutrients:** An electric pressure cooker cooks food at a higher pressure but lower temperature than oven or stovetop cooking methods. The steam cooking process locks in the nutrients in food and preserves them better than the other cooking methods.

6. **You get more intense flavors:** Pressure cooking releases a gentle heat that allows the spices to release their natural oils and aromas, and the end result is a combination of flavors that makes it seem as if the recipe has been slow-cooking for hours.

7. **There's no odor:** Most curry recipes use strong and aromatic spices that permeate the entire house, including clothes and upholstery. The sealing technique in the electric pressure cooker locks in those aromas, creating no to very minimal external odor.

8. **It doesn't heat up the house:** In the summer, running the oven can really heat up the house. Cooking in the pressure cooker can achieve similar results without heating up the house.

Types of Electric Pressure Cookers

Due to the recent rise in popularity of electric pressure cookers, there are currently many different brands and models to choose from. Here are some of the most popular models for readers who are new to electric pressure cooking.

While varying in size, most of these electric pressure cookers can perform the following basic functions: pressure cook, slow cook, cook rice, sauté/brown, steam, and keep warm.

Instant Pot Lux: Available in 3-quart, 6-quart, and 8-quart sizes, this is the entry-level product from the Instant Pot brand. I consider this the best version for everyday users if you don't care about a yogurt function and low-pressure setting. Latest models also include cake and egg maker functions.

Instant Pot Duo: Available in 3-quart, 6-quart, and 8-quart sizes, this is the number one bestseller on Amazon. A great cooker for beginners, it includes the yogurt function, while the low-pressure setting allows more control over cooking delicate food such as seafood and vegetables.

Instant Pot Ultra: This model is for the advanced cook and includes 21 preset temperature options and a sous vide feature. It also offers the altitude adjustment preset, which is great for those living in high altitude. The winning feature is its self-sealing lid, which eliminates the chance of your forgetting to seal it. It is available in 3-quart, 6-quart, and 8-quart sizes.

Mealthy Multipot 2.0: Available in a 6-quart size, this model is comparable to the Instant Pot Ultra or Duo Plus. Its winning feature is the hands-free and programmable pressure release with the touch of a button. With it, you

Electric Pressure Cooker Terminology

All these electric pressure cookers have many buttons and functions that do different things, so getting started with electric pressure cookers or multi-cookers can seem intimidating.

But don't worry—it's much easier than it seems. Here is a list of buttons and functions that are common across most electric pressure cookers (the first three are ones that I use most for making curry).

» **Pressure Cook/Manual:** This is the most used button. It defaults to high pressure (which can be changed to low) and you use [+] and [−] to set the cook time.

» **Sauté:** It defaults to the normal or medium heat setting and takes 30 to 40 seconds for the pot to get hot. Use the default normal/medium setting for sautéing veggies, adjust to more/high for browning meats, and adjust to less/low to simmer.

» **Keep Warm/Cancel:** Turns on or off the automatic keep warm function. By default, it is set to on. This button is also used to end a cooking program.

» **Rice:** This button defaults to 12 minutes at low pressure and is used for cooking white rice.

» **Steam:** This button cooks at high pressure for 10 minutes (normal), 15 minutes (high), or 3 minutes (less). In most models, you have to use an external timer for cooking.

» **Slow Cook:** Slow cook on low, normal, or high. Use [+] and [−] to increase or decrease the cook time (temperature defaults may vary with different models).

In addition, here are a few terms you will come across in the world of electric pressure cooking:

» **Natural Pressure Release (NPR or NR):** After the cooking cycle ends, let the pot release the pressure on its own. This can take anywhere from 5 to 30 minutes, depending on the cooking time.

» **Quick Pressure Release (QR or QPR):** After the cooking cycle ends, use the pressure cooker's instructions to manually release pressure. Very hot steam is released during this process, so follow the recommended safety precautions.

» **Low Pressure and High Pressure** (**LP and HP):** Most recipes call for high pressure, which is the default for most pressure cook/manual presets. Low-pressure settings are more suitable for cooking delicate items such as seafood and vegetables.

» **Pot in Pot (PIP):** A method used to cook another item or a side dish (like rice) in the same pot as the curry or entrée by using a metal trivet. The trivet (or rack) sits at the bottom of the inner pot with a 1-to-3-inch clearance, depending on its height. Another bowl or dish is set on top of it, while the curry cooks in the main pot.

» **Deglaze:** Using liquid to scrape off the brown bits of aromatics (or meat) that may have stuck to the bottom of the pot while cooking. This prevents the "burn" sign during pressure cooking.

can choose between a natural, quick, and auto release of steam. As of now, this is the only cooker that offers this feature. All Mealthy models come with a set of commonly used accessories as well.

Ninja Foodi: Available in 3-quart, 6.5-quart, and 8-quart sizes, this pressure cooker offers the same set of features as its competitors. Its winning feature is the TenderCrisp technology, which allows the latest model of the Ninja Foodi to double as an air fryer, with an interchangeable lid.

Crockpot Express: Available in a 6-quart size, this pressure cooker includes the same features, including slow cook, pressure cook, sauté, steam, yogurt maker, rice, and warm. It comes with a nonstick inner pot versus a stainless-steel one, which is the default for most competitors.

Essential Equipment

While the electric pressure cooker is the star of the show in my kitchen—and this book—there are a handful of other kitchen tools that help make it easier to cook curry. These are the underdogs of the kitchen world because, no matter how awesome a dish turns out, they never get mentioned. The following are some essential pieces of equipment my curry kitchen cannot do without:

Spice Grinder/Coffee Grinder: I have a basic, under-$20 coffee grinder dedicated to grinding spices. Some curries tend to come to life with freshly ground spices, so this tiny grinder comes in handy for grinding those small quantities.

Mini Food Processor: I call this my sous chef. It takes only a few pulses to chop onions, finely chop ginger, garlic, and chilies, and crush or puree tomatoes. In less than half the time and effort, this mini food processor can prep your ingredients for you.

Immersion Blender: Some of the popular curries require the sauce to be pureed after cooking for a smooth end texture. Immersion blenders, also known as stick blenders, enable you to blend hot curry right in the pot itself without having to wait for it to cool down. The same results can be achieved with countertop blenders as well, but for safety reasons, wait for the curry to cool down to blend.

Trivet: It's a stainless-steel rack that creates a platform for placing another bowl in the cooker, without coming in contact with the contents of the main pot. It works great for steaming and pot-in-pot cooking. Most current electric pressure cookers ship with this accessory.

About the Recipes

In addition to a wide variety of globally inspired curry dishes, the recipes in this book include everything from spice blends to sides and anything else you'll need for a well-rounded curry meal. While the world offers a much larger selection of curries, I've covered recipes that are well known and more familiar to many of us.

The recipe chapters are broken out by region, so you can flip to the section that interests you the most. Meatless recipes are either marked vegetarian or vegan, and we've also labeled gluten-free, dairy-free, and nut-free recipes. Toward the end, you'll find a chapter for spice blends and curry pastes that form the foundation of these diverse curries, along with grain and rice side dishes to complete a meal.

All these recipes have been tested multiple times in my 6-quart Instant Pot or Mealthy Multipot, but I have tried my best to keep the instructions as generic as possible to fit any electric pressure cooker brand you have.

All recipes use standard US metrics (cups and spoon measurements). We've also included a measurement conversion chart (page 171) if you need one.

These recipes were developed to be easily recreated by home cooks of all skill levels, from beginners to the more experienced. They will satisfy your takeout cravings in less time than it takes for you to order in, and they're definitely healthier and cheaper than the restaurant alternatives. All right, then—let's get cooking!

A Note about Cooking Time

The total time on these recipes factors in preparation, sautéing, pressure-cooking time, **10 minutes for pressure building**, pressure release times (natural or quick), and any finishing steps.

Although I suggest a **10-minute prep time** for most recipes, which could involve chopping aromatics, making a spice paste, and/or pureeing tomatoes, the actual time varies depending on individual working pace.

If a recipe calls for **natural pressure release**, the total time can vary between 5 and 20 minutes, depending on the cooking time, quantity, and your specific pressure cooker brand. All recipes in this book factor in either a **timed natural release** or a **quick-release**, which takes about one minute.

Most of these recipes can be made in 45 minutes or less from start to finish, with a chunk of that being hands-off cooking time (pressure build, pressure cook, and pressure release time). There are a few recipes that take 60 minutes or longer because they either require marinating the meat or soaking ingredients. Even though soaking or marinating is "inactive cooking time," it has been mentioned in each recipe under "prep" and the total time accounts for that.

SPICY LAMB CURRY, PAGE 32

CHAPTER 2

THE INDIAN SUBCONTINENT

I t would not be an exaggeration to say that the Indian subcontinent has been a curry hub since the 1500s. The modern-day Indian subcontinent consists of seven countries: India, Pakistan, Bangladesh, Sri Lanka, Maldives, Nepal, and Bhutan. But from a culinary point of view, it is divided into the Northern and Southern regions. The distinctions are primarily based on two factors: spices and ingredients used in regional curries, and the accompanying starch (rice or roti).

One can find many overlaps in curries from the countries in the Northern region, including Pakistan, Northern India, Nepal, and Bhutan, with a heavy influence of local climate, terrain, and the Mughal Empire.

Bangladesh shares its flavor profile with West Bengal in India, collectively called Bengali cuisine, in which fresh fish, mustard, and poppy seeds are used in many curries.

Curries from the Southern region—including the southern coast of India, Maldives, and Sri Lanka—typically contain shredded coconut, coconut milk, curry leaves, mustard seeds, and various chilies and spices to season their curries.

While it is impossible to include all regional curries from the Indian subcontinent in this book (that would be a book in itself), the following are some traditional and popular curries you might have tasted in a restaurant or at a friend's home!

Butter Chicken // MURGH MAKHANI

GLUTEN-FREE • NUT-FREE

Serves:
5

Prep Time:
15 minutes,
includes time
to marinate

Cook Time:
8 minutes
(2 minutes
on sauté,
6 minutes on
high pressure)

Release:
Natural
release for
10 minutes,
followed by
quick

Total Time:
45 minutes

Butter Chicken, or Murgh Makhani, was invented by accident in the 1950s at Moti Mahal Restaurant in New Delhi as a way to soften leftover grilled chicken. Traditionally, this recipe is made in two steps: grilling and simmering. Chicken is marinated in spiced yogurt overnight, then grilled and simmered in a mild, creamy tomato sauce seasoned with toasted Indian spices. A light drizzle of heavy cream toward the end gives this dish its iconic rich and creamy taste. Here's an easy one-pot pressure cooker variation for a restaurant-style Butter Chicken.

FOR THE MARINADE

¼ cup plain Greek or thick yogurt

2 teaspoons minced ginger

2 teaspoons minced garlic

½ teaspoon salt

½ teaspoon turmeric powder

1 teaspoon Kashmiri red chili powder (or paprika plus a pinch of cayenne)

1 teaspoon Garam Masala (page 150)

1 teaspoon coriander powder

Juice of ½ lime

1½ pounds boneless skinless chicken thighs, fat trimmed and halved

FOR THE SAUCE

1 tablespoon ghee or unsalted butter

1 tablespoon minced ginger

1 tablespoon minced garlic

1 (14.5-ounce) can diced tomatoes or 3 to 4 ripe Roma tomatoes

½ teaspoon turmeric powder

½ teaspoon Kashmiri red chili powder

2 teaspoons Garam Masala (page 150)

2 teaspoons coriander powder

1 teaspoon cumin powder

½ cup water (more as needed)

½ cup heavy whipping cream

1 teaspoon dried fenugreek leaves

½ teaspoon sugar (optional)

2 tablespoons chopped cilantro (for garnish)

1. For the marinade, in a large mixing bowl, combine the yogurt, ginger, garlic, salt, turmeric, chili powder, garam masala, coriander, and lime juice. Add the chicken and coat well. Refrigerate while you prepare other ingredients and start the sauce.

2. Preheat the electric pressure cooker by selecting sauté. When the inner pot is hot, after about 30 seconds, add the ghee. Stir in the ginger and garlic and cook until they start to sizzle.

3. Add the tomatoes, turmeric, chili powder, Garam Masala, coriander, and cumin and stir for 1 minute. Turn off sauté. Add water and scrape off any brown bits that may have stuck to the bottom.

4. Place the marinated chicken in the sauce. Don't stir.

5. Lock the lid into place. Select manual or pressure cook and adjust to high, then cook for 6 minutes on sealing mode.

6. When the cooking is complete, wait 10 minutes for natural pressure release, after which follow the quick-release method as per your cooker instructions. Unlock and remove the lid.

7. Remove the chicken and cut it into bite-size pieces. Using an immersion blender, purée the sauce in the pot. Add the chicken back to the sauce.

8. Select sauté. Stir in the heavy cream, fenugreek leaves, and sugar (if using) and simmer for 2 to 3 minutes. Garnish with fresh cilantro and serve warm with Cumin Rice (page 160) or Roti (page 162).

Chicken Korma // KORMAH

GLUTEN-FREE

Serves:
6

Prep Time:
10 minutes

Cook Time:
18 minutes
(10 minutes
on sauté,
8 minutes on
high pressure)

Release:
Natural
release for
10 minutes,
followed by
quick

Total Time:
50 minutes

Korma is a dish from Mughal cuisine that originated in the Indian subcontinent around the 16th century. The word "korma" comes from the Urdu word "kormah" meaning "braising." In this mild curry found in most Indian and Pakistani restaurants, meat or vegetables are braised in yogurt, cream, or a nut paste and seasoned with mild aromatic Indian spices like cardamom, cinnamon, and coriander.

FOR THE NUT PASTE

½ cup water

2 tablespoons
slivered almonds

2 tablespoons cashews

FOR THE SAUCE

2 tablespoons ghee or olive oil

1 teaspoon cumin seeds

2 bay leaves

1 medium onion,
finely chopped

1 tablespoon minced ginger

1 tablespoon minced garlic

½ cup puréed tomato or
2 tablespoons tomato paste

½ cup plain yogurt,
whisked smooth

1 teaspoon salt

2 teaspoons Garam Masala
(page 150)

1 tablespoon coriander
powder

1 teaspoon cumin powder

¼ teaspoon turmeric

¼ teaspoon red chili powder
or cayenne

½ cup water (more as needed)

2 pounds chicken
breast (whole)

½ teaspoon cardamom
powder or crushed seeds
(for finishing)

2 tablespoons chopped fresh
cilantro (for garnish)

1. To make the nut paste, in a microwave-safe bowl, heat the water, almonds, and cashews for 5 minutes. Set aside to cool. When cool, blend to a smooth paste.

2. To make the sauce, preheat the electric pressure cooker by selecting sauté, and adjust to high. When the inner pot is hot, after about 30 seconds, put in the ghee, cumin seeds, and bay leaves.

3. When the cumin seeds begin to sizzle, add the onion and cook for 7 to 8 minutes, until they begin to brown.

4. Add the ginger and garlic and cook for another minute.

5. Add pureed tomato, nut paste, whisked yogurt, and all the spices, and sauté for a minute.

6. Turn off sauté. Add water and scrape off any brown bits that may have stuck to the bottom. Add the chicken breast, pushing it under the sauce.

7. Lock the lid in place. Select manual or pressure cook and adjust to high. Cook for 8 minutes on sealing mode.

8. When the cooking is complete, wait 10 minutes for natural pressure release, after which follow the quick-release method as per your cooker instructions. Unlock and remove the lid.

9. Remove the chicken breast and cut it into bite-size pieces. Add the chicken back in the sauce and stir in the cardamom.

10. Garnish with fresh chopped cilantro and serve with steamed Basmati Rice (page 157) or Roti (page 162).

Chicken Tikka Masala

GLUTEN-FREE

Serves:
5

Prep Time:
10 minutes

Cook Time:
15 minutes
(9 minutes
on sauté,
6 minutes on
high pressure)

Release:
Natural
release for
10 minutes,
followed by
quick

Total Time:
45 minutes

Chicken Tikka Masala is the British cousin of the popular Punjabi Butter Chicken. I took this classic restaurant-style recipe, which requires multiple steps and cooking methods, and made it easier by assembling the whole dish in the same pot.

FOR THE MARINADE

2 tablespoons plain
Greek yogurt

2 teaspoons minced garlic

2 teaspoons minced ginger

1 teaspoon salt

½ teaspoon turmeric powder

1½ teaspoons Kashmiri red
chili powder or paprika

1 teaspoon Garam Masala
(page 150)

1 teaspoon coriander powder

2 teaspoons freshly squeezed
lime juice

1½ pounds boneless skinless
chicken thighs, fat trimmed

FOR THE CURRY

2 tablespoons olive oil
(divided)

1 medium onion, coarsely
chopped

1 tablespoon minced ginger

1 tablespoon minced garlic

⅓ cup cashews

1 (14.5-ounce) can diced
tomatoes or 3 to 4 ripe Roma
tomatoes

1 teaspoon salt

1 teaspoon turmeric powder

2 teaspoons Garam Masala
(page 150)

2 teaspoons coriander powder

1 teaspoon cumin powder

1½ teaspoons Kashmiri red
chili powder or paprika

¼ teaspoon cardamom
powder

3 tablespoons plain Greek
yogurt, whisked smooth

½ cup water (or as needed)

2 teaspoons dried fenugreek
leaves

½ teaspoon sugar or honey   ¼ cup heavy whipping cream
                                  (optional)

1. To make the marinade, combine all ingredients listed for
the marinade and toss the chicken in until well coated.
Refrigerate while you prepare the other ingredients.

2. Preheat the electric pressure cooker by selecting sauté.
When the inner pot is hot, after about 30 seconds, add
1 tablespoon of oil. Add the marinated chicken and cook it
for one minute on each side to seal in the marinade flavors.
Remove the chicken and set aside.

3. Add the remaining oil, along with the onion, ginger, garlic,
and cashews, stir and cook for 3 minutes. Add the tomatoes,
salt, turmeric, garam masala, coriander, cumin, Kasmiri red
chili powder, cardamom, and yogurt and cook for another
minute. Turn off sauté. Add water and scrape off any brown
bits stuck on the bottom. Place the chicken back in the pot.

4. Lock the lid in place. Select manual or pressure cook and
adjust to high. Cook for 6 minutes on sealing mode.

5. When the cooking is complete, wait 10 minutes for natural
pressure release, after which follow the quick-release method
as per your cooker instructions. Unlock and remove the lid.

6. Remove the chicken and cut it into bite-size pieces. Using
an immersion blender, purée the sauce in the pot to a smooth
consistency.

7. Select sauté. Add the chicken pieces and dried fenugreek
leaves and simmer for 2 to 3 minutes.

8. Stir in sugar. To make creamier, add heavy whipping cream
(if using) and simmer for 2 minutes. Serve warm.

Sri Lankan-Style Chicken Curry // KUKUL MAS

DAIRY-FREE • GLUTEN-FREE

Serves:
5

Prep Time:
10 minutes

Cook Time:
20 minutes
(10 minutes
on sauté,
10 minutes on
high pressure)

Release:
Natural
release for
10 minutes,
followed by
quick

Total Time:
40 minutes

This delicious and spicy chicken curry, called kukul mas, is one of the most popular dishes from the exotic island nation of Sri Lanka. Bone-in chicken is coated and cooked with warming spices like coriander, fennel, cardamom, and curry and gets its deep red color and heat from paprika and cayenne. Coconut milk cuts through the heat and brings this curry to life. The following is my take on a traditional Sri Lankan classic.

FOR THE SPICE RUB

1 teaspoon salt

½ teaspoon turmeric

1 tablespoon coriander powder

1 tablespoon curry powder

½ teaspoon fennel powder

¼ teaspoon ground cinnamon

1 teaspoon cardamom powder

1 tablespoon paprika

½ teaspoon cayenne powder

1 tablespoon apple cider vinegar

1½ pounds chicken drumsticks, skin removed

FOR THE SAUCE

2 tablespoons coconut oil

1 medium onion, chopped

8 to 10 curry leaves

1 tablespoon minced ginger

5 garlic cloves, minced

2 tablespoons tomato paste

½ cup coconut milk

¾ cup water

2 tablespoons chopped cilantro (for garnish)

1. To make the spice rub, in a mixing bowl, mix together the salt, turmeric, coriander, curry powder, fennel powder, cinnamon, cardamom, paprika, cayenne, and vinegar. Using kitchen shears, remove the skin from the chicken drumsticks and toss them in the spice rub. Set them aside while you prepare other ingredients and start the sauce.

2. Preheat the electric pressure cooker by selecting sauté and adjust to high. When the inner pot is hot, after about 30 seconds, pour in the oil, onion, and curry leaves and cook for 5 minutes, stirring in between.

3. Add the ginger, garlic, chicken, and tomato paste, and cook for 4 to 5 minutes, stirring in between.

4. Turn off sauté. Add the coconut milk and water and scrape off any brown bits that may have stuck to the bottom.

5. Lock the lid in place. Select manual or pressure cook and adjust to high. Cook for 10 minutes on sealing mode.

6. When the cooking is complete, wait 10 minutes for natural pressure release, after which follow the quick-release method as per your cooker instructions. Unlock and remove the lid.

7. Garnish with cilantro and serve with steamed Basmati Rice (page 157).

TIP: This recipe uses coconut oil, which contributes to the authentic flavors of the curry. However, you can substitute any clear oil, such as avocado or light olive oil, for the coconut oil. If you cannot find curry leaves, substitute ½ teaspoon of lime zest.

Chicken and Lentil Curry // DHANSAK

GLUTEN-FREE

Serves:
6

Prep Time:
10 minutes,
including time
to soak lentils

Cook Time:
13 minutes
(7 minutes
on saute,
6 minutes on
high pressure)

Release:
Natural for
10 minutes,
followed by
quick

Total Time:
43 minutes

Dhansak curry came from the Parsi community when immigrants from Persia settled in Western India around the 8th century CE. Their dishes combined elements of Persian and Gujarati cuisine. Dhansak is made by cooking meat with lentils and vegetables and is served with rice. Traditionally, it is a 2-step process, in which lentils are cooked separately and then simmered with the meat stew. In this easy one-pot recipe, the lentils and chicken cook together, making it doable on a weeknight, too.

½ cup green lentils

2 tablespoons olive oil or ghee

1 medium onion, finely chopped

1 tablespoon minced ginger

1 tablespoon minced garlic

2 Roma tomatoes, chopped

1 tablespoon tomato paste

2 teaspoons dried fenugreek leaves

1 teaspoon salt, adjust to taste

1 teaspoon turmeric powder

2 teaspoons Garam Masala (page 150)

1 tablespoon coriander powder

1 teaspoon cumin powder

1½ teaspoons Kashmiri red chili powder or paprika

1½ pounds boneless skinless chicken thighs, fat trimmed and halved

1 cup cubed pumpkin or butternut squash

1 cup water

Squeeze of lime (for finishing)

2 tablespoons chopped cilantro (for garnish)

1. Rinse and soak lentils in warm water for 10 minutes.

2. Preheat the electric pressure cooker by selecting sauté. When the inner pot is hot, after about 30 seconds, pour in the olive oil and chopped onions and cook for 5 minutes, until they start turning light golden brown.

3. Stir in the ginger, garlic, tomatoes, tomato paste, fenugreek leaves, salt, turmeric, garam masala, coriander, cumin, and Kashmiri red chili powder and continue to cook for another 2 minutes.

4. Add the chicken pieces, rinsed and drained lentils, pumpkin, and water, and give it a stir. Scrape off any brown bits that may have stuck to the bottom. Turn off sauté.

5. Lock the lid in place. Select manual or pressure cook and adjust to high. Cook for 6 minutes on sealing mode.

6. When the cooking is complete, wait 10 minutes for natural pressure release, after which follow the quick-release method as per your cooker instructions. Unlock and remove the lid.

7. Squeeze in the lime juice and garnish with cilantro. Serve with Cumin Rice (page 160).

TIP: I use green lentils in this recipe because they hold their shape after pressure cooking, but if you prefer a softer texture, replace green lentils with red lentils and follow the same directions.

Bengali-Style Chicken Curry // REZALA

GLUTEN-FREE

Serves:
5

Prep Time:
20 minutes
includes
marinating
time

Cook Time:
20 minutes
(14 minutes
on saute,
6 minutes on
high pressure)

Release:
Natural
release for
10 minutes,
followed by
quick

Total Time:
1 hour

Rezala is a mildly seasoned, creamy curry in which meat or chicken is cooked in a yogurt- and nut-based sauce. A dish once cooked exclusively in the royal kitchens of the Mughal Nawabs (rulers), it became accessible to the commoners after India's partition in 1947. Even today, it continues to be a delicacy in West Bengal and Bangladesh, the eastern food hub of the Indian subcontinent.

FOR THE MARINADE

1½ pounds chicken drumsticks, skin removed

2 tablespoons plain Greek yogurt

1 tablespoon minced ginger

1 tablespoon minced garlic

1 medium onion, chopped in chunks

1 teaspoon salt

1 teaspoon white pepper powder

1 teaspoon Garam Masala (page 150)

FOR THE NUT PASTE

10 cashews

2 teaspoons white poppy seeds (*khus khus*) or white sesame seeds

¼ cup boiling water

FOR THE SAUCE

2 tablespoons ghee

1 small onion, sliced thin

3 to 4 whole red chiles or ½ teaspoon red pepper flakes

1 teaspoon Garam Masala (page 150)

1 teaspoon coriander powder

½ teaspoon white pepper

¼ cup plain Greek yogurt, whisked until smooth

½ cup water (or as needed)

½ teaspoon saffron strands

½ teaspoon sugar

2 tablespoons chopped cilantro (for garnish)

1. To make the marinade, in a food processor, combine all ingredients listed for the marinade (except the chicken) and blend to a smooth paste. In a bowl, add the paste to the chicken and refrigerate while you prepare the other ingredients.

2. Soak the cashews and poppy seeds in the boiling water for 10 minutes. Using a blender, grind the mixture to a smooth paste. Remove and put aside.

3. To make the sauce, preheat the electric pressure cooker by selecting sauté. When the inner pot is hot, after about 30 seconds, add the ghee, onion, and red chiles. Cook for about 8 minutes, stirring in between, until onions start browning. Add the nut paste and stir.

4. Stir in chicken with all the marinade. Add the remaining garam masala, coriander, and white pepper and continue to cook for another 5 minutes, stirring in between.

5. Add the yogurt while stirring continuously. Scrape off any brown bits that may have stuck to the bottom of the pot. Add the water and stir. Turn off sauté.

6. Lock the lid in place. Select manual or pressure cook and adjust to high. Cook for 6 minutes on sealing mode.

7. When the cooking is complete, wait 10 minutes for natural pressure release, after which follow the quick-release method as per your cooker instructions. Unlock and remove the lid.

8. Stir in the saffron and sugar, and garnish with cilantro. Serve with Cumin Rice (page 160).

Spicy Chicken with Peppers // JALFREZI

DAIRY-FREE • GLUTEN-FREE • NUT-FREE

Serves:
5

Prep Time:
10 minutes

Cook Time:
10 minutes
(7 minutes
on sauté,
3 minutes on
high pressure)

Release:
Natural
release for
5 minutes,
followed by
quick

Total Time:
35 minutes

Jalfrezi is a semidry curry that originated in the Bengal region of "British India" as a way to use up leftovers by frying them with chiles and onion. Jalfrezi is made by stir-frying chicken (or paneer) with onions and peppers and served in thick, spicy gravy. Here's a quick pressure cooker version, in which we accomplish the same depth of flavors and texture as an authentic Chicken Jalfrezi.

2 tablespoons olive oil (divided)

1 medium onion, thinly sliced

½ red bell pepper, sliced

½ green bell pepper, sliced

2 jalapeños, crowns removed

1 teaspoon cumin seeds

1 tablespoon minced ginger

1 tablespoon minced garlic

½ cup Roma tomato, chopped

2 tablespoons tomato paste

¾ teaspoon salt

½ teaspoon turmeric

1 tablespoon coriander

¼ teaspoon red chili powder

1½ pounds chicken breast, halved and cut into ½-inch slices

2 tablespoons chopped cilantro, plus 2 additional tablespoons for garnish

½ cup water

1. Preheat the electric pressure cooker by selecting sauté. When the inner pot is hot, after about 30 seconds, pour in 1 tablespoon of oil, the onions, bell peppers, and jalapeños. Cook for 3 to 5 minutes, until the onions and peppers soften a little. Remove and reserve for later.

2. Add the remaining tablespoon of olive oil followed by the cumin seeds.

3. When the cumin begins to sizzle, add the ginger and garlic and cook for 1 minute.

4. Add the tomato, tomato paste, salt, turmeric, coriander, chili powder, chicken, and chopped cilantro along with the water. Stir everything and turn off sauté.

5. Lock the lid in place. Select manual or pressure cook and adjust to high. Cook for 3 minutes on sealing mode.

6. When the cooking is complete, wait 5 minutes for natural pressure release, after which follow the quick-release method as per your cooker instructions. Unlock and remove the lid.

7. Select sauté to reduce the sauce. When the sauce reaches your desired consistency, add back in the reserved peppers, onions, and jalapeño, and garnish with cilantro. Enjoy with steamed Basmati Rice (page 157).

TIP: Sautéing peppers and onions and adding them back after pressure cooking helps them retain their crunch and makes for an authentic Jalfrezi curry. For a softer texture, pressure cook them with the chicken. Additionally, this recipe can be made vegetarian by swapping paneer for the chicken.

Lamb Curry with Caramelized Onions // BHUNA GOSHT

GLUTEN-FREE • NUT-FREE

Serves:
5

Prep Time:
10 minutes

Cook Time:
35 minutes
(15 minutes
on saute,
20 minutes
on high
pressure)

Release:
Natural
release for
10 minutes,
followed by
quick

Total Time:
1 hour
5 minutes

Bhuna Gosht, which translates to "sautéed meat," is a popular mutton preparation in India and Pakistan, in which meat is sautéed and then cooked with caramelized onions, fresh ginger, and garlic, and seasoned with aromatic toasted garam masala. The cooked curry is simmered until the gravy reduces and the color darkens. This restaurant-style Bhuna Gosht tastes great with naan, Roti (page 162) or Cumin Rice (page 160).

3 tablespoons ghee or oil

2 bay leaves

2 medium onions, sliced

¼ teaspoon salt

1½ pounds boneless leg of lamb, cut into 2-inch pieces

1 tablespoon minced ginger

1 tablespoon minced garlic

2 teaspoons Garam Masala (page 150), plus additional ½ teaspoon for finishing

1 tablespoon coriander powder

1 teaspoon cumin powder

¼ teaspoon turmeric

1 teaspoon Kashmiri red chili powder

1 teaspoon salt

2 tablespoons tomato paste

3 tablespoons plain Greek yogurt

½ cup water (or as needed)

½ teaspoon ground cardamom

3 tablespoons chopped cilantro (for garnish)

1. Preheat the electric pressure cooker by selecting sauté and adjust to high. When the inner pot is hot, after about 30 seconds, put in the ghee. Add the bay leaves and onions with ¼ teaspoon salt to help them brown faster. Cook onions for 6 to 8 minutes, until brown.

2. Add the lamb pieces, ginger, and garlic, stir and cook for another 3 minutes.

3. Add 2 teaspoons of Garam Masala, the coriander, cumin, turmeric, Kashmiri red chili powder, salt, and tomato paste. Stir and cook for 1 minute.

4. Whisk the yogurt until smooth and add it to the pot while stirring. Scrape off any brown bits that may have stuck to the bottom, adding water as needed. Turn off sauté.

5. Lock the lid in place. Select manual or pressure cook and adjust to high. Cook for 20 minutes on sealing mode.

6. When the cooking is complete, wait 10 minutes for natural pressure release, after which follow the quick release method as per your cooker instructions. Unlock and remove the lid.

7. Select sauté. Add the ground cardamom and reserved ½ teaspoon garam masala and simmer for 4 to 5 minutes until the gravy reduces and thickens.

8. Garnish with cilantro and serve with Roti (page 162) or Cumin Rice (page 160).

TIP: Another popular meat choice for this curry is goat stew meat. To use that, cut goat meat in 2-inch pieces, follow the recipe directions, and increase the cooking time to 30 minutes, followed by a natural pressure release.

Goan Lamb Vindaloo

GLUTEN-FREE • NUT-FREE

Serves:
5

Prep Time:
15 minutes

Cook Time:
32 minutes
(12 minutes
on sauté,
20 minutes
on high
pressure)

Release:
Natural
release for
10 minutes,
followed by
quick

Total Time:
1 hour
7 minutes

Vindaloo is an Indian adaptation of the Portuguese dish, Carne de Vinha D'alhos, meaning "meat marinated in wine and garlic." The infusion of chilies, which were introduced in Goa by the Portuguese, with local Indian spices gives this dish its signature taste. In this easy recipe, lamb pieces are pressure cooked with a spice paste made of mild red chilies, aromatics, spices, and apple cider vinegar. Apple cider vinegar adds a sweet tart taste, which mimics the taste of the traditionally used palm vinegar.

FOR THE MARINADE

6 to 7 Kashmiri red chiles

1 teaspoon cumin seeds

1 teaspoon mustard seeds

2 tablespoons coriander seeds

1-inch cinnamon stick

½ teaspoon whole black peppercorns

6 cloves

5 green cardamom pods

6 garlic cloves

1-inch ginger, peeled

1 tablespoon apple cider vinegar

½ teaspoon brown sugar

1 teaspoon salt

¼ cup water

1½ pounds boneless lamb leg or shoulder, cut into 2-inch pieces

FOR THE SAUCE

2 tablespoons oil

1 large onion, finely chopped

1 cup water

¼ cup chopped fresh cilantro (for garnish)

1. Soak the red chiles in boiling water for 10 minutes, while you prepare the other ingredients.

2. To make the marinade, drain the chiles and add them to a blender along with the cumin, mustard, coriander, cinnamon, peppercorns, cloves, cardamom, garlic, ginger, vinegar, brown sugar, salt, and water and blend to a smooth paste.

3. In a large mixing bowl, combine lamb pieces with the marinade and set aside while you start the sauce.

4. Preheat the electric pressure cooker by selecting sauté and adjust to high. When the inner pot is hot, after about 30 seconds, pour in the oil and onions and cook for 5 minutes. Keep stirring in between.

5. Add the lamb along with the marinade, stir and cook for 3 minutes.

6. Turn off sauté. Add the water and deglaze the pot to scrap off any brown bits from the bottom.

7. Lock the lid in place. Select manual or pressure cook and adjust to high. Cook for 20 minutes on sealing mode.

8. When the cooking is complete, wait 10 minutes for natural pressure release, after which follow the quick-release method as per your cooker instructions. Unlock and remove the lid.

9. Select sauté and simmer for 4 to 5 minutes, until the sauce thickens to your desired consistency.

10. Garnish with cilantro and serve over steamed Basmati Rice (page 157), or with Roti (page 162).

TIP: To enhance the flavor of this dish, marinate the lamb for 30 minutes to overnight.

Red Lamb Curry // LAAL MAAS

GLUTEN-FREE • NUT-FREE

Serves:
5

Prep Time:
15 minutes

Cook Time:
35 minutes
(15 minutes
on Sauté,
20 minutes
on high
pressure)

Release:
Natural
Release for
10 minutes,
followed by
quick

Total Time:
1 hour
10 minutes

Laal Maas is a meat curry from the colorful state of Rajasthan, India. Pieces of meat are cooked in a sauce made of yogurt, garam masala, and local dried red chile peppers, called Mathania Mirch. This dish is typically spicy and has a thin gravy. In this recipe, I use dried Kashmiri red chilies, which are easier to source, to mimic the look and taste of this traditional curry. Laal Maas is best served warm with whole-wheat roti.

FOR THE MARINADE

1 tablespoon coriander seeds

1 tablespoon Garam Masala (page 150)

4 green cardamom pods

¼ teaspoon cinnamon powder

6 garlic cloves

1-inch ginger, peeled

½ teaspoon turmeric

1 teaspoon salt

10 dried Kashmiri red chiles, soaked in ½ cup hot water for 10 minutes

½ cup plain Greek or thick yogurt

1½ pounds boneless lamb leg or shoulder, cut into 2-inch pieces

FOR THE SAUCE

3 tablespoons ghee

1 bay leaf

1 large onion, finely chopped (1½ cups)

1 cup water

2 tablespoons chopped cilantro (for garnish)

1. To make the marinade, in a food processor, pour in the coriander, Garam Masala, cardamom, cinnamon, garlic, ginger, turmeric, salt, and soaked red chiles with liquid and blend to make a smooth paste. Add yogurt and blend again until smooth.

2. Marinate lamb pieces in this paste and set aside while you prepare the other ingredients and start the sauce.

3. Preheat the electric pressure cooker by selecting sauté and adjust to high. When the inner pot is hot, after about 30 seconds, put in the ghee, bay leaf, and onions. Cook for 7 to 8minutes, until onions are brown.

4. Add the marinated meat, stir, and cook for 5 minutes. Turn off sauté.

5. Add the water and give it a stir. Scrape off any brown bits that may have stuck to the bottom.

6. Lock the lid in place. Select manual or pressure cook and adjust to high. Cook for 20 minutes on sealing mode.

7. When the cooking is complete, wait 10 minutes for natural pressure release, after which follow the quick-release method as per your cooker instructions. Unlock and remove the lid.

8. Select sauté and simmer for 2 to 3 minutes, until the sauce thickens to your desired consistency.

9. Garnish with cilantro and serve with Roti (page 162).

TIP: Kashmiri red chilies have a mild flavor and are used to give a bright reddish-brown color to this curry. If you prefer to make this curry mild, substitute 2 tablespoons of regular paprika powder for the Kashmiri chilies. Additionally, to enhance the flavor of this dish, marinate the lamb for 30 minutes to overnight.

Spicy Lamb Curry // ROGAN JOSH

GLUTEN-FREE • NUT-FREE

Serves:
5

Prep Time:
10 minutes

Cook Time:
35 minutes
(15 minutes
on sauté,
20 minutes
on high
pressure)

Release:
Natural
release for
10 minutes,
followed by
quick

Total Time:
1 hour
5 minutes

Rogan Josh is one of the signature curries of the Kashmiri multicourse meal known as Wazwan from the picturesque northern tip of India. It is an aromatic curry made by cooking lamb or goat meat in a spicy yogurt sauce, flavored with toasted garam masala, fennel, and cardamom. It gets its iconic reddish-brown color from local dried red chilies, the Kashmiri red chiles. Here's an easy restaurant-style version of a traditional Kashmiri curry.

FOR THE SPICE PASTE

¼ cup plain yogurt

2 teaspoons Garam Masala (page 150)

1-inch ginger, peeled

½ teaspoon fennel powder

½ teaspoon crushed black pepper

1 teaspoon salt

2 teaspoons Kashmiri red chili powder

2 teaspoons paprika

FOR THE SAUCE

3 tablespoons ghee

1 bay leaf

1 medium onion, sliced thin

1½ pounds boneless lamb leg or shoulder cut into 2-inch pieces

½ teaspoon saffron

¾ cup water

¼ cup plain yogurt

¼ teaspoon crushed cardamom

½ teaspoon Garam Masala (page 150)

2 tablespoons chopped cilantro (for garnish)

1. To make the spice paste, in a small mixing bowl, mix together yogurt, Garam Masala, ginger, fennel, black pepper, salt, Kashmiri red chili powder, and paprika and whisk to combine.

2. Preheat the electric pressure cooker by selecting sauté and adjust to high. When the inner pot is hot, after about 30 seconds, put in the ghee, bay leaf, and onion. Cook for 7 to 8 minutes, until brown.

3. Add the lamb pieces and the spice paste, then stir and cook for 5 minutes.

4. Add the saffron and water and give it a stir. Turn off sauté. Scrape off any brown bits that may have stuck to the bottom.

5. Lock the lid in place. Select manual or pressure cook and adjust to high. Cook for 20 minutes on sealing mode.

6. When the cooking is complete, wait 10 minutes for natural pressure release, after which follow the quick-release method as per your cooker instructions. Unlock and remove the lid.

7. Select sauté to simmer the sauce. In a separate bowl, whisk the yogurt until smooth and mix in one ladle of hot curry from the pot to temper the yogurt. Add the yogurt-curry mix back to the pot and stir until it's incorporated.

8. Stir in the crushed cardamom and garam masala and simmer for 2 minutes. Turn off sauté.

9. Garnish with cilantro and serve with steamed Basmati Rice (page 157).

TIP: A traditional home-style Rogan Josh has a thinner curry that is made without onions. To make that, skip the step of browning onions and follow the remaining instructions.

Chettinad Shrimp Curry

GLUTEN-FREE

Serves:
4

Prep Time:
10 minutes

Cook Time:
10 minutes
(7 minutes
on sauté,
3 minutes on
low pressure)

Release:
Quick

Total Time:
30 minutes

This delicious curry comes from the Chettinad region of Tamil Nadu state in India. Chettinad curry is one of the most popular dishes in Southern Indian cuisine, which uses a variety of freshly ground spices, curry leaves, and coconut to create a unique flavor. In this take on a traditional recipe, I make a curry base by blending tomatoes with toasted red chiles, coconut, and an assortment of whole warming spices, then cook the shrimp in it.

FOR THE SPICE PASTE

8 cashews

¼ cup desiccated coconut or ⅓ cup shredded unsweetened coconut flakes

1 tablespoon coriander seeds

1 teaspoon fennel seeds

1 teaspoon cumin seeds

½ teaspoon black peppercorns

5 whole dried red chilies (cayenne or Mexican)

4 green cardamom pods

5 cloves

1-inch cinnamon bark

2 garlic cloves, crushed

1 tablespoon grated ginger

2 Roma tomatoes

¼ cup water

FOR THE SAUCE

2 tablespoons oil

1 medium onion, finely chopped

8 to 10 curry leaves

¾ teaspoon salt (adjust to taste)

¼ teaspoon turmeric

½ teaspoon freshly squeezed lime juice

1 pound raw shrimp, extra-large (21 to 30 count per pound), thawed if frozen

½ cup water

3 to 4 tablespoons chopped cilantro (for garnish)

1. Select sauté and adjust to low. Put in the cashews, coconut, coriander, fennel, cumin, peppercorns, chilies, cardamom, cloves, cinnamon, and garlic. Toast them for 2 to 3 minutes, until the coconut begins to turn a light golden color. Keep stirring in between to prevent burning.

2. Turn off sauté and transfer the ingredients to blender. Add the ginger and tomatoes, and blend to make a smooth paste. Add water as needed.

3. Wipe the pot clean to remove any bits of coconut or spices that may have stuck. Select sauté and adjust to medium to make the sauce. When the inner pot is hot, after about 30 seconds, add the oil, onions, and curry leaves. Cook for 3 to 4 minutes, until the onions become translucent.

4. Add the spice paste, salt, and turmeric and cook for a minute. Add the shrimp and water and turn off sauté.

5. Lock the lid in place. Select manual or pressure cook and adjust to low. Cook for 3 minutes on sealing mode.

6. When the cooking is complete, follow the quick-release method as per your cooker instructions to release the pressure. Unlock and remove the lid.

7. Squeeze in a few drops of fresh lime juice and season to taste. Garnish with cilantro and serve with steamed Basmati Rice (page 157).

TIP: This is a relatively spicy curry. To tone down the level of spice, use just two of the whole dried chilies and deseed them before adding.

Coconut Fish
Curry // MEEN MOLEE/MOILEE

DAIRY-FREE • GLUTEN-FREE

Serves:
4

Prep Time:
15 minutes,
includes
marinating
time for fish

Cook Time:
5 minutes
(3 minutes
on sauté,
2 minutes on
low pressure)

Release:
Quick

Total Time:
30 minutes

Meen Molee is a mildly spiced fish and coconut stew from the coastal Indian state of Kerala. This curry is also very popular in Malaysia and Singapore. "Meen" means fish in Malayalam, the local language of Kerala, and "Moilee" refers to a simple stew. Unlike most other curries originating from Kerala, which tend to be spicy, this one is lightly seasoned with mild spices like coriander and white pepper, then finished with a squeeze of fresh lime or lemon juice.

FOR THE MARINADE

½ teaspoon turmeric

¾ teaspoon salt

¼ teaspoon red chili flakes

½ teaspoon white pepper

1 tablespoon freshly squeezed lime or lemon juice

1 pound Alaskan cod or mahi-mahi fish fillets cut into 2-inch pieces

FOR THE SAUCE

2 tablespoons coconut oil or avocado oil

1 teaspoon mustard seeds

10 to 12 curry leaves

1 cup thinly sliced shallots

1 tablespoon minced ginger

1 tablespoon minced garlic

2 whole serrano chiles or jalapeños

2 teaspoons coriander powder

½ teaspoon white pepper powder

2 cups coconut milk

½ to 1 teaspoon freshly squeezed lime or lemon juice

1. To make the marinade, combine the turmeric, salt, red chili flakes, white pepper, and lime juice and coat the fish pieces in it. Set aside for 15 minutes while you prepare the other ingredients.

2. Preheat the electric pressure cooker by selecting sauté. When the inner pot is hot, after about 30 seconds, pour in the oil, mustard seeds, and curry leaves.

3. When they begin to splutter, add shallots, ginger, garlic, and serrano chilies, and cook for 3 to 4 minutes, until the shallots soften and turn translucent.

4. Add the coriander powder, white pepper, coconut milk, and fish pieces and give it a stir. Turn off sauté.

5. Lock the lid in place. Select manual or pressure cook and adjust to low. Cook for 2 minutes on sealing mode.

6. When the cooking is complete, follow the quick-release method as per your cooker instructions to release the pressure. Unlock and remove the lid.

7. Squeeze in a few drops of fresh lime or lemon juice and check for seasoning. Serve warm with steamed Basmati Rice (page 157).

TIP: The same directions will work for other fish varieties like salmon and tilapia as long as fillets are 2 inches wide and less than 1 inch in thickness.

Egg Curry // ANDA CURRY

GLUTEN-FREE

Serves:
4

Prep Time:
10 minutes

Cook Time:
10 minutes
(6 minutes
on sauté,
4 minutes on
high pressure)

Release:
Quick

Total Time:
30 minutes

This simple and delicious curry made with hard-boiled eggs is a popular street food, as well as staple in many homes. Different regions in India and Pakistan have their own variations of the curry. This recipe is a typical Punjabi-style egg curry, in which boiled eggs get dunked in a spicy tomato-onion gravy and served with hot paratha, roti, or steamed rice. Using this recipe, you can boil the eggs and make the curry in the same pot in 30 minutes. Surprised? Try it!

2 tablespoons olive oil

1 bay leaf

1 teaspoon cumin seeds

½ teaspoon mustard seeds

1 cup chopped onion

2 whole serrano chiles

1 tablespoon minced ginger

1 tablespoon minced garlic

1 teaspoon salt

½ teaspoon turmeric

½ teaspoon Kashmiri red chili powder

2 teaspoons coriander powder

½ teaspoon dried fenugreek

1 teaspoon Garam Masala (page 150)

1 cup chopped Roma tomatoes

1 cup water

6 large eggs

2 tablespoons heavy whipping cream (optional)

2 tablespoons chopped cilantro (for garnish)

1. Preheat the electric pressure cooker by selecting sauté and adjust to high. When the inner pot is hot, after about 30 seconds, add the oil, bay leaf, cumin, and mustard seeds.

2. When those begin to sizzle and splutter, add the onions, serrano chiles, ginger, and garlic, and cook for 3 to 4 minutes, until the onions become soft.

3. Stir in salt, turmeric, Kashmiri red chili powder, coriander, fenugreek, garam masala, and tomatoes and cook for another 2 to 3 minutes. Turn off sauté. Add the water and stir.

4. To make hard-boiled eggs in the same pot, place the eggs in a steamer basket or on a metal trivet, and place that in the pot with the curry. Be sure to use a basket or stand that has legs and is elevated above the curry.

5. Lock the lid in place. Select manual or pressure cook and adjust to high. Cook for 4 minutes on sealing mode.

6. When the cooking is complete, follow the quick-release method as per your cooker instructions to release the pressure. Unlock and remove the lid.

7. Remove the eggs and put them in a bowl of cold water with ice for 5 minutes. Using an immersion blender, purée the curry in the pot. Skip this step if you don't want a smooth curry. Stir in heavy whipping cream (if using) and let it rest for 1 minute. Transfer the curry to a serving bowl.

8. Peel the eggs. Using a fork, poke each egg in multiple places. Cut them in half and place the eggs cut-side up in the curry. Garnish with cilantro and serve with Roti (page 162) or steamed Basmati Rice (page 157).

TIP: If you don't have a steamer basket or a trivet, you can make the hard-boiled eggs on the stovetop. Place eggs in a saucepan and fill it with enough water to cover the eggs. Turn the heat to medium-high and cook for 10 to 12 minutes, depending on the heat level. Turn off the heat and place the eggs in an ice bath for 5 minutes. Peel the eggs and follow the remaining instructions.

Creamy Mixed Lentils // LANGARWALI DAL

VEGETARIAN • GLUTEN-FREE • NUT-FREE

Serves:
4

Prep Time:
10 minutes

Cook Time:
45 minutes
(5 minutes
on sauté,
40 minutes
on high
pressure)

Release:
Natural
release for
10 minutes,
followed by
quick

Total Time:
1 hour
15 minutes

This simple yet satisfying lentil curry is a staple of the free meals, called "Langar," served by the community kitchen in a Gurdwara, the place of worship for Sikhs. The traditional recipe combines two varieties of lentils and slow cooks them with onions, ginger, garlic, tomatoes, and mild Indian spices, until the lentils break down and get creamy naturally. This easy pressure cooker recipe achieves the same comforting textures and flavors with much less effort.

½ cup whole urad dal (black matpe beans)

¼ cup chana dal (split chickpeas)

3 tablespoons ghee

1 teaspoon cumin seeds

1 cup finely chopped onion

1 tablespoon minced ginger

2 garlic cloves, minced

2 serrano chilies, seeded and finely chopped

1 cup chopped Roma tomatoes

¾ teaspoon salt

½ teaspoon turmeric

1 teaspoon Kashmiri red chili powder

1 teaspoon Garam Masala (page 150)

2 teaspoons coriander powder

1 teaspoon cumin powder

¼ cup chopped cilantro, plus an additional 3 tablespoons for garnish

1¾ cups water

1 to 2 teaspoons butter (optional)

1. Wash and soak urad and chana dal in warm water while you prepare other ingredients and start the onions.

2. Preheat the electric pressure cooker by selecting sauté. When the inner pot is hot, after about 30 seconds, add the ghee and cumin seeds.

3. When the cumin begins to sizzle, add the onion, ginger, garlic, and serrano chiles, then stir and cook for 2 minutes.

4. Add the tomatoes, salt, turmeric, Kashmiri red chili powder, garam masala, coriander, and cumin and stir and cook for 3 minutes, until the tomatoes break down.

5. Rinse and drain the soaked lentils and add them to the pot. Add the cilantro and water. Stir, scraping off any brown bits stuck to the bottom. Turn off sauté.

6. Lock the lid in place. Select manual or pressure cook and adjust to high. Cook for 40 minutes on sealing mode.

7. When the cooking is complete, wait 10 minutes for natural pressure release, after which follow the quick-release method as per your cooker instructions. Unlock and remove the lid.

8. Stir the lentils and mash a few beans using a potato masher. This gives a creamy texture and thickens the curry. Stir in the butter (if using) to enhance creaminess.

9. Garnish with the reserved cilantro and serve with Roti (page 162) or Cumin Rice (page 160).

TIP: If you cannot find black lentils, use brown lentils instead and reduce the pressure cooking time to 12 minutes.

Tangy Chickpea Curry // PUNJABI CHOLE

VEGETARIAN • GLUTEN-FREE • NUT-FREE

Serves:
6

Prep Time:
10 minutes

Cook Time:
13 minutes
(8 minutes
on sauté,
5 minutes on
high pressure)

Release:
Natural
release for
5 minutes,
followed by
quick

Total Time:
38 minutes

Punjabi Chole, or Amritsari Chole, is a street food version of the popular Indian and Pakistani curry Chana Masala. In addition to the commonly used warm spices, this North Indian chickpea curry uses dried mango powder to get its iconic tangy taste, while whole tea bags create the deep brown color. The curry is finished with a tangy seasoning, called Chaat Masala, and the street version is served with a baked flatbread called kulcha, while the homestyle curry is typically enjoyed with Roti (page 162) or rice.

---

2 tablespoons ghee

2 bay leaves

1 large onion, finely chopped

1 tablespoon minced ginger

2 serrano chilies, seeded and finely chopped

1 tablespoon tomato paste or 1 Roma tomato, seeded and chopped

1¾ teaspoons black salt or regular salt

2 teaspoons cumin powder

1½ tablespoons coriander powder

1 teaspoon fennel powder

1 tablespoon Garam Masala (page 150)

2 teaspoons dry mango powder (amchur)

1 teaspoon Kashmiri red chili powder

2 (15-ounce) cans of chickpeas, rinsed and drained

1½ cups water

1 Indian tea bag or English Breakfast tea bag

1 teaspoon chaat masala

1 teaspoon julienned ginger

3 tablespoons chopped cilantro (for garnish)

1. Preheat the electric pressure cooker by selecting sauté. When the inner pot is hot, after about 30 seconds, add the ghee, bay leaves, and onion. Cook for 5 minutes, until the onions soften.

2. Add the ginger and serrano chilies and sauté another 2 minutes.

3. Add the tomato paste, salt, cumin, coriander, fennel, Garam Masala, mango powder, and Kashmirir red chili powder, then stir and cook another minute. Add the chickpeas and water and stir well. Add the tea bag and gently push it down into the liquid. Turn off sauté.

4. Lock the lid in place. Select manual or pressure cook and adjust to high. Cook for 5 minutes on sealing mode.

5. When the cooking is complete, wait 5 minutes for natural pressure release, after which follow the quick-release method as per your cooker instructions. Unlock and remove the lid.

6. Using a fork or potato masher, mash a few beans and stir. This gives a creamy texture and thickens the curry.

7. Add the chaat masala and ginger and stir.

8. Garnish with cilantro and serve with Roti (page 162) or Cumin Rice (page 160).

Creamy Vegetable Curry // NAVRATAN KORMA

VEGETARIAN • GLUTEN-FREE

Serves:
5

Prep Time:
15 minutes

Cook Time:
7 minutes
(6 minutes
on sauté,
1 minute on
low pressure)

Release:
Quick

Total Time:
35 minutes

Navratan Korma is a rich vegetable curry made with nine ingredients. "Navratan" means "nine gems" and "korma" means "braised stew," so this name basically translates to "braised stew of the nine gems." This curry combines four kinds of vegetables with nuts and dried fruits, then braises them in a rich yogurt-based sauce. A staple in many Indian restaurants, this curry is surely the tastiest way to eat your vegetables.

FOR THE KORMA PASTE

10 to 12 raw cashews

2 tablespoons slivered almonds

1 tablespoon poppy seeds or cashews

1 medium onion, chopped

¾ cup water

1-inch ginger, peeled

5 garlic cloves

FOR THE SAUCE

2 tablespoons ghee (divided)

2 tablespoons golden raisins

1 tablespoon slivered almonds

1 tablespoon cashew halves

2 bay leaves

2 cups cauliflower florets

1 cup carrots, cut into ½-inch pieces

1 cup gold potato, cut into 1-inch cubes

¾ cup green beans, cut into 1-inch pieces

1 cup paneer, cut into 1-inch pieces

¾ teaspoon salt

1 teaspoon Garam Masala (page 150)

1 teaspoon coriander powder

1 teaspoon white pepper

½ cup plain yogurt

½ cup water

½ cup heavy cream (for finishing)

¼ teaspoon sugar

½ teaspoon cardamom powder

1. To make korma paste, in a microwave-safe bowl, put the cashews, almonds, poppy seeds, onion, water, ginger, and garlic and heat for 4 minutes. Let it cool for a few minutes. Using a food processor, make a smooth paste and put it aside.

2. Preheat the electric pressure cooker by selecting sauté. When the inner pot is hot, after about 30 seconds, add 1 tablespoon ghee and the raisins, almonds, and cashews. Sauté for 1 to 2 minutes until the raisins plump up and the nuts turn golden in color (not brown). Remove promptly to prevent burning and set aside for garnish.

3. Add the remaining 1 tablespoon ghee, bay leaves, and korma paste. Sauté for 4 to 5 minutes to cook off the raw flavors.

4. Add the cauliflower, carrots, potato, green beans, paneer, salt, garam masala, coriander, and white pepper then stir. Whisk the yogurt until smooth and mix it in while stirring. Add the water and stir. Turn off sauté.

5. Lock the lid in place. Select manual or pressure cook and adjust to low. Cook for 1 minute on sealing mode.

6. When the cooking is complete, follow the quick-release method as per your cooker instructions to release the pressure. Unlock and remove the lid.

7. Stir in the heavy whipping cream, sugar, and cardamom powder. Let it sit 3 to 5 minutes. Garnish with the reserved nuts and raisins and serve with Cumin Rice (page 160).

Paneer in Creamy Tomato Sauce // PANEER MAKHANI

VEGETARIAN • GLUTEN-FREE

Serves:
4

Prep Time:
10 minutes

Cook Time:
9 minutes
(5 minutes
on sauté,
4 minutes on
high pressure)

Release:
Quick

Total Time:
29 minutes

Paneer Makhani, also known as Paneer Butter Masala, is a sweet and creamy curry from the Indian subcontinent. This restaurant favorite is a vegetarian variation of the internationally famous Butter Chicken. In this easy 30-minute recipe, firm Indian cottage cheese, called paneer, is simmered in a mildly seasoned tomato sauce and finished with a touch of heavy cream and dried fenugreek leaves. Enjoy it with steamed Basmati Rice (page 157) or store-bought butter naan!

---

1 tablespoon ghee or unsalted butter

1 tablespoon minced ginger

1 tablespoon minced garlic

¼ to ½ cup water (as needed)

1 (14-ounce) can diced tomatoes, puréed

¾ teaspoon salt

½ teaspoon turmeric powder

½ teaspoon Kashmiri red chili powder

1 teaspoon paprika

2 teaspoons Garam Masala (page 150)

1 tablespoon coriander powder

14 ounces paneer, cut into ½-inch cubes

½ cup heavy whipping cream

1 tablespoon dried fenugreek leaves

1 teaspoon sugar (adjust to taste)

2 to 3 tablespoons fresh chopped cilantro (for garnish)

1. Preheat the electric pressure cooker by selecting sauté. When the inner pot is hot, after about 30 seconds, add the ghee, ginger, and garlic and cook for 1 minute.

2. Add the water and scrape off any brown bits that may have stuck to the bottom. Add the puréed tomato, salt, sugar, turmeric, Kashmiri red chili powder, paprika, Garam Masala, and coriander. Stir well and cancel sauté.

3. Lock the lid in place. Select manual or pressure cook and adjust to high. Cook for 4 minutes on sealing mode.

4. When the cooking is complete, follow the quick-release method as per your cooker instructions to release the pressure. Unlock and remove the lid.

5. Select sauté. Stir in the paneer cubes, heavy whipping cream, sugar, and dried fenugreek leaves. Let it simmer 3 to 4 minutes until the paneer softens and sauce thickens to your liking. Turn off sauté.

6. Garnish with cilantro and serve with Roti (page 162) or Cumin Rice (page 160).

TIP: Canned diced tomatoes give the most consistent results in this recipe. If using fresh tomatoes instead, use 3 to 4 ripe Roma tomatoes and purée them. To make this curry dairy-free, substitute coconut oil and for the ghee replace heavy cream with coconut cream and paneer with extra-firm tofu.

Paneer and Spinach Curry // PALAK PANEER

VEGETARIAN • GLUTEN-FREE

Serves:
4

Prep Time:
10 minutes

Cook Time:
6 minutes
(6 minutes
on sauté,
0 minutes on
high pressure)

Release:
Quick

Total Time:
26 minutes

Palak Paneer, or Saag Paneer, is a popular curry originating in the northern region of the Indian subcontinent. In this simple and delicious curry, soft paneer cubes are simmered in flavorful spinach gravy, which is made by cooking spinach with aromatics and toasted warm spices, then puréed. In this easy recipe, we leverage the pressure cooker to infuse these flavors into the spinach while preserving its gorgeous green color and nutrients in just "0" minutes of pressure cooking time. Surprised? What that means is that the curry is done cooking in the time it takes the cooker to reach pressure!

1 tablespoon ghee or olive oil

1 teaspoon cumin seeds

1 medium onion, sliced

½ tablespoon minced ginger

1 tablespoon minced garlic

1 serrano chile, seeded and halved

1 teaspoon salt

½ teaspoon turmeric powder

1 teaspoon Garam Masala (page 150)

2 teaspoons coriander powder

1 teaspoon cumin powder

½ teaspoon Kashmiri red chili powder

10 to 12 ounces baby spinach, washed and dried

1 cup water

10 ounces paneer, cubed into ½-inch pieces

1 teaspoon butter

1. Preheat the electric pressure cooker by selecting sauté. When the inner pot is hot, after about 30 seconds, add the oil and cumin seeds.

2. When the cumin seeds begin to sizzle, add the onions, ginger, garlic, and chile pepper and cook for about 3 minutes, until onions turn translucent.

3. Add the salt, turmeric, Garam Masala, coriander, cumin, and Kashmiri red chili powder and stir well. Add the baby spinach and water and give it a stir. Cancel sauté.

4. Lock the lid in place. Select manual or pressure cook and adjust to high. Cook for 8 minutes on sealing mode.

5. When the cooking is complete, follow the quick-release method as per your cooker instructions to release the pressure. Unlock and remove the lid.

6. Using an immersion blender, purée the spinach mix. If the quantity doesn't seem enough to submerge the immersion blender, lift and tilt the pot to purée.

7. Turn on sauté. Stir in the paneer cubes and simmer for 2 minutes until the paneer cubes become soft. Turn off sauté.

8. Stir in the butter. This adds a silky-smooth finish to the sauce and gives it a gorgeous shine. Serve hot with Cumin Rice (page 160) or Roti (page 162).

TIP: Palak and Saag are often used interchangeably. While "palak" means spinach in Hindi, "saag" refers to a variety of green leafy vegetables, including spinach, mustard greens, fenugreek, collard greens, and other similar varieties.

Spicy Vegetable Curry // PAV BHAJI

VEGETARIAN • GLUTEN-FREE • NUT-FREE

Serves:
8

Prep Time:
10 minutes

Cook Time:
10 minutes
(2 minutes
on sauté,
8 minutes on
high pressure)

Release:
Quick

Total Time:
30 minutes

Pav Bhaji is a popular Indian street food from Mumbai, Maharashtra. In this simple and flavorful dish, a spicy vegetable mash called bhaji is seasoned with a complex spice blend called pav bhaji masala and served with butter-toasted bread rolls, called pav. Pav bhaji masala is available in Indian grocery stores or online. A dollop of butter, chopped onions, cilantro, and a squeeze of lemon juice are what complete this dish. Try this easy, almost "dump and cook" recipe, and enjoy the flavors of Mumbai in less than 30 minutes.

2 tablespoons butter, plus 1 to 2 teaspoons for garnish

1 medium onion, chopped, plus an additional ½ cup for finishing

1 cup green bell pepper, chopped

1 tablespoon minced ginger

1 tablespoon minced garlic

2 cups chopped Roma tomatoes

2 tablespoons tomato paste

2½ tablespoons pav bhaji masala

2 teaspoons paprika

2 teaspoons salt

1 cup water, divided

1 cup carrots, chopped in ½-inch pieces

3 cups cubed gold potatoes

2 cups cauliflower florets

½ cup green beans, cut into 1-inch pieces

½ cup green peas (frozen or fresh)

Juice of ½ lemon

¼ cup chopped onion (for garnish)

¼ cup chopped cilantro (for garnish)

1. Preheat the electric pressure cooker by selecting sauté. When the inner pot is hot, after about 30 seconds, add the butter. When the butter melts, add the onion, bell pepper, ginger, and garlic, and cook for 2 minutes.

2. Add the tomatoes, tomato paste, Pav Bhaji Masala, paprika, salt, and ¼ cup of water. Stir until everything is combined.

3. Turn off sauté. Add the carrots, potatoes, cauliflower, green beans, and green peas and toss until coated in the spice mix. Add the remaining water.

4. Lock the lid in place. Select manual or pressure cook and adjust to high. Cook for 8 minutes on sealing mode.

5. When the cooking is complete, follow the quick-release method as per your cooker instructions to release the pressure. Unlock and remove the lid.

6. Using a potato masher, mash the vegetables until they are the consistency of a thick curry. (If the curry seems to loose, turn on sauté and simmer for 2 to 3 minutes.)

7. Stir in the lemon juice and adjust seasoning.

8. Serve the bhaji warm, topped with butter, onion, and cilantro, with butter-toasted dinner rolls.

TIP: To add protein to this curry, stir in 3 ounces paneer (crumbled or chopped into ¼-inch pieces) after pressure cooking and simmer it for 2 to 3 minutes.

Lentils and Vegetable Curry // SAMBAR

VEGAN • VEGETARIAN • GLUTEN-FREE • NUT-FREE

Serves:
4

Prep Time:
10 minutes

Cook Time:
15 minutes
(5 minutes
on sauté,
10 minutes on
high pressure)

Release:
Natural
release for
5 minutes,
followed by
quick

Total Time:
45 minutes

Sambar, also called Saambar, is a lentil and vegetable-based curried stew in which split pigeon peas are cooked in a spicy tomato and tamarind broth and flavored with a unique spice blend, called Sambar powder. Mustard seeds and curry leaves add a citrusy aroma to the tangy curry, which is served with steamed rice, and other South Indian preparations like idli (steamed rice and lentil cakes), vada (lentil fritters), or dosa (lentil and rice crispy crepes). The combination of vegetables and lentils makes this a balanced curry ideal for weeknight cooking.

½ cup toor dal (split pigeon peas)

1 tablespoon olive oil

1 teaspoon mustard seeds

12 to 15 curry leaves

1 medium onion, chopped into ½-inch pieces

2 teaspoons minced ginger

2 teaspoons minced garlic

1 cup chopped Roma tomatoes

¾ to 1 teaspoon salt

½ teaspoon turmeric powder

1 tablespoon Sambar powder

1 teaspoon coriander powder

1 large zucchini, cut into 1-inch pieces

1 large carrot, cut into ½-inch pieces

1 turnip or white daikon, cut into 1-inch pieces

2 cups water

1 teaspoon tamarind concentrate

2 tablespoons chopped cilantro (for garnish)

1. Rinse and soak toor dal in hot water while you prepare other ingredients.

2. Turn on sauté on high. Add the oil and heat for 30 seconds. Add the mustard seeds.

3. When the mustard seeds begin to splutter, add the curry leaves, onion, ginger, and garlic. Sauté for 3 minutes, until the onions soften a little.

4. Add the tomatoes, salt, turmeric, Sambar, and coriander. Sauté for 2 minutes till the tomatoes break down.

5. Add the rinsed and drained lentils along with the chopped zucchini, carrot, and turnip. Add the water and stir. Turn off sauté.

6. Lock the lid in place in sealing position. Set pressure cook or manual for 10 minutes at high pressure on sealing mode.

7. When the cooking time is up, let the pressure release naturally for 5 minutes, followed by a quick release as per your cooker instructions. Unlock and remove the lid.

8. Add tamarind concentrate and stir. Use the back of a ladle or potato masher and mash the lentils to make them creamy. Let the curry rest for 2 to 3 minutes. Adjust the seasoning according to the recipe tip. Garnish with cilantro and serve with steamed Basmati Rice (page 157).

TIP: The taste and texture of Sambar can vary by region. Here are a few ways to customize it: For a softer texture, adjust pressure cook time to 12 minutes. Optionally, add ¼ to ½ teaspoon of sugar to add a sweet touch. Reduce Sambar powder to 2 teaspoons to make it mild or increase to 1 ½ tablespoons to make it spicier. Add more tamarind concentrate to make it tangier.

Kidney Bean Curry // RAJMA

VEGAN • VEGETARIAN • GLUTEN-FREE • NUT-FREE

Serves:
4

Prep Time:
10 minutes

Cook Time:
10 minutes
(5 minutes
on sauté,
5 minutes on
high pressure)

Release:
Natural
release for
5 minutes,
followed by
quick

Total Time:
35 minutes

Another common vegan curry from the Indian Subcontinent, Rajma is a kidney bean curry with a thick onion-tomato-based sauce, seasoned with garam masala and other warm spices. Even though this curry is traditionally made with red kidney beans, using this versatile pressure cooker recipe, you can make it with dark beans, pinto, or any other variety of kidney beans. Combined with steamed Basmati Rice (page 157), it makes for a popular comfort food, called Rajma Chawal, in most Punjabi homes.

1 tablespoon olive oil

1 teaspoon cumin seeds

1 medium onion, finely chopped

1 serrano chile, seeded and finely chopped

1 tablespoon minced ginger

1 tablespoon minced garlic

1 cup chopped Roma tomatoes

¾ teaspoon salt

½ teaspoon turmeric powder

1 teaspoon Garam Masala (page 150)

2 teaspoons ground coriander

1 teaspoon roasted ground cumin

½ teaspoon Kashmiri red chili powder

2 (15-ounce) cans kidney beans, rinsed and drained

1½ cups water

2 tablespoons chopped cilantro (for garnish)

1. Preheat the electric pressure cooker by selecting sauté. When the inner pot is hot, after about 30 seconds, add the oil and cumin seeds.

2. When the cumin seeds begin to sizzle (a few seconds), add the onion and chile and cook for 3 minutes, stirring in between.

3. Stir in the ginger and garlic and cook another minute.

4. Add the tomatoes and the salt, turmeric, Garam Masala, coriander, cumin, and Kashmiri red chili powder, then stir and cook for a minute, until the tomatoes soften.

5. Add the rinsed and drained kidney beans to the pot. Add the water and stir.

6. Lock the lid in place. Select manual or pressure cook and adjust to high. Cook for 5 minutes on sealing mode.

7. When the cooking is complete, wait 5 minutes for natural pressure release, after which follow the quick-release method as per your cooker instructions. Unlock and remove the lid.

8. Using a fork or potato masher, mash a few beans and stir. This gives a creamy texture and thickens the curry.

9. Garnish with cilantro and serve with steamed Basmati Rice (page 157).

TIP: This recipe can be made with dried kidney beans as well. Soak 2 cups beans in 4 cups water overnight or for 8 hours. Rinse and drain and add as per recipe directions along with an additional cup of water. Pressure cook for 35 minutes, followed by a natural pressure release.

SPICY CHICKEN WITH PEPPERS, PAGE 24

CAMBODIAN-STYLE FISH CURRY, PAGE 90

CHAPTER 3

THAILAND & OTHER ASIAN COUNTRIES

When you think of your favorite curry, a Thai variety probably comes to mind. But curry has been a part of almost all Asian cuisines since the 18th century, thanks to trade, colonization, and the famous Silk Route. From Japan to Malaysia, almost every Asian country has its own signature curry.

In late 18th century, when the British established the Straits Settlements at Penang, Malacca, and Singapore, they brought curry powder with them. Soon after, the kitchens in Hong Kong, Singapore, and Thailand incorporated it into recipes along with local ingredients and created new dishes like the Cantonese *Gah-Lay* and the Thai *Kaeng Kari*, to name two. A common way to categorize Thai curry is by the color of the curry paste used to make the dish.

The British Royal Navy introduced curry to Japan in the late 18th century, where it gained popularity as a Western dish. The Japanese army and navy adapted it to their tastes and adopted it as convenient canteen food, spreading it through the country.

Most Asian-style curries use Indian spices like turmeric, coriander, and cumin and a spice paste for flavor. Many consist of hearty vegetables and seasonal produce, and they are often served with rice to complete the meal.

Thai Green Curry with Chicken // GAENG KIEW WAN GAI

DAIRY-FREE • GLUTEN-FREE

Serves:
5

Prep Time:
15 minutes,
includes time
to prepare
curry paste

Cook Time:
7 minutes
(2 minutes
on sauté,
5 minutes on
low pressure)

Release:
Natural
release for
5 minutes
followed by
quick

Total Time:
37 minutes

This sweet and spicy aromatic curry is from central Thailand and perhaps the most unique among all Asian curries. Its traditional name, Gaeng Kiew Wan, translates to "curry green sweet." The green comes from the Bird's Eye chilies used to make the paste, and the sweetness comes from the coconut cream and palm sugar. Enjoy this delicious curry using homemade or store-bought green curry paste in just a little over 30 minutes.

---

1 (14-ounce) can coconut milk (unshaken)

2 ounces Green Curry Paste (page 156), or store-bought

1½ pounds boneless skinless chicken thighs, cut into 1-inch pieces

2 teaspoons fish sauce or light soy sauce

2 teaspoons palm sugar or brown sugar

6 kaffir lime leaves or 1 teaspoon lime zest

1 (4-ounce) can bamboo shoots

2 medium carrots, peeled and cut at an angle into ¼-inch slices

½ cup Thai basil leaves

1 to 2 teaspoons freshly squeezed lime juice (adjust to taste)

1. Preheat the electric pressure cooker by selecting sauté. When the inner pot is hot, after about 30 seconds, add 3 tablespoons of the thick cream from the top of the coconut milk can.

2. When it starts to bubble, stir in the curry paste and cook for a minute, until the mix thickens.

3. Add the remaining coconut milk and stir until combined.

4. Add the chicken pieces, fish sauce, sugar, lime leaves, bamboo shoots, and carrots. Give it a stir and turn off sauté.

5. Lock the lid in place. Select manual or pressure cook and adjust to low. Cook for 5 minutes on sealing mode.

6. When the cooking is complete, wait 5 minutes for natural pressure release, after which follow the quick-release method as per your cooker instructions. Unlock and remove the lid.

7. Stir in the Thai basil leaves and lime juice and serve with steamed brown or white Jasmine Rice (page 158).

TIP: To make this curry spicier, add 3 to 4 ounces of curry paste. Another popular variation of this curry is made with pork. To use that instead of chicken, simply cut the pork in ½-inch-thick strips and add along with other ingredients. Pressure cook for 5 minutes on high pressure and let the pressure release naturally.

Thai Red Curry with Shrimp // KAENG PHET KUNG

DAIRY-FREE • GLUTEN-FREE

Serves:
4

Prep Time:
15 minutes,
includes time
to prepare
curry paste

Cook Time:
4 minutes
(1 minute
on sauté,
3 minutes on
low pressure)

Release:
Quick

Total Time:
30 minutes

Thai Red Curry, or Kaeng Phet, is perhaps the most popular Thai curry. The base of this dish is an aromatic spice paste made with dried red chiles, lemongrass, kaffir lime leaves, lemon juice, shallots, coriander, and cumin and is the same paste used in many other Thai curries. In this preparation, we cook it with coconut milk, shrimp, and bell peppers and finish the curry with sugar and a splash of lime.

1 (14-ounce) can coconut milk (unshaken)

2 ounces Red Curry Paste (page 154), or store-bought

2 teaspoons fish sauce or light soy sauce

1 to 2 teaspoons palm sugar or brown sugar

1 pound raw peeled and deveined extra-large shrimp, 21 to 30 per pound

½ red bell pepper, thinly sliced

1 teaspoon freshly squeezed lime juice

¼ cup Thai basil or sweet basil leaves

1. Preheat the electric pressure cooker by selecting sauté. When the inner pot is hot, after about 30 seconds, add 3 tablespoons of the thick cream from the top of the coconut milk can.

2. When it starts to bubble, stir in the curry paste and cook for a minute, until the mix thickens.

3. Add the remaining coconut milk and stir until combined. Add the fish sauce, sugar, shrimp, and bell peppers and stir. Turn off sauté.

4. Lock the lid in place. Select manual or pressure cook and adjust to low. Cook for 3 minutes on sealing mode.

5. When the cooking is complete, follow the quick-release method as per your cooker instructions to release the pressure. Unlock and remove the lid.

6. Stir in the lime juice and basil and serve with brown or white Jasmine Rice (page 158).

TIP: If using frozen shrimp, for best results thaw them overnight in the refrigerator. Add smaller shrimp after the pressure cooking is complete and simmer on sauté until they cook through and turn opaque, about 3 to 5 minutes.

Thai Yellow Curry with Chicken and Potatoes // GAENG GAREE GAI

DAIRY-FREE • GLUTEN-FREE

Serves:
5

Prep Time:
15 minutes,
includes time
to prepare
curry paste

Cook Time:
8 minutes
(3 minutes
on sauté,
5 minutes on
low pressure)

Release:
Natural
Release for
5 minutes
followed by
quick

Total Time:
38 minutes

Thai Yellow Curry is another well-known curry in Thai cuisine. The mildest of them all, this curry paste consists of dried red chiles, lemongrass, ginger, garlic, and Indian curry powder, which is where the curry gets its yellow color. Typically made with chicken and potatoes, the subtle flavors in this curry make it an ideal base for fish, seafood, and tofu. Served with steamed Jasmine Rice (page 158), this curry is pure comfort in a bowl!

1 (14-ounce) can coconut milk (unshaken)

3 ounces Yellow Curry Paste (page 155), or store-bought

1½ pounds boneless skinless chicken breast or thighs cut into 1-inch pieces

1 small onion, cut into 1-inch chunks

1 cup gold potatoes, cut into 1-inch cubes

1 cup carrots, cut into 1-inch pieces

2 teaspoons fish sauce, or light soy sauce

1 to 2 teaspoons palm sugar, or brown sugar

1. Preheat the electric pressure cooker by selecting sauté. When the inner pot is hot, after about 30 seconds, add 3 tablespoons of the thick cream from the top of the coconut milk can.

2. When it starts to bubble, stir in the curry paste and cook for a minute, until the mix thickens.

3. Add the chicken and onion and sauté another minute.

4. Stir in the remaining coconut milk. Add the potatoes, carrots, fish sauce, and sugar and stir. Turn off sauté.

5. Lock the lid in place. Select manual or pressure cook and adjust to low. Cook for 5 minutes on sealing mode.

6. When the cooking is complete, wait 5 minutes for natural pressure release, after which follow the quick-release method as per your cooker instructions. Unlock and remove the lid.

7. Serve warm with steamed brown or white Jasmine Rice (page 158).

TIP: It is easy to customize this curry by adding your preferred vegetables. Some popular choices include sweet potato, bell peppers, button mushrooms, pumpkin, and squash. If using delicate vegetables like snow peas or broccoli, add them after pressure cooking and simmer for 2 to 3 minutes until they soften.

Thai Panang Curry with Pork // KAENG PHANAENG NEUA

DAIRY-FREE • GLUTEN-FREE

Serves:
4

Prep Time:
15 minutes,
includes time
to make curry
paste

Cook Time:
10 minutes
(5 minutes
on Saute,
5 minutes on
high pressure)

Release:
Natural
release for
5 minutes
followed by
quick

Total Time:
40 minutes

Panang Curry, also called "phanang" or "penang," has a nutty peanut flavor. To make this sweet and savory curry, a spice paste made with dried red chiles, lemongrass, kaffir lime leaves, Thai ginger, shallots, coriander, cumin, and roasted peanuts is cooked with coconut milk. Creamy unsalted peanut butter stirred in before pressure cooking helps achieve the signature creamy and nutty flavors in this curry.

1 (14-ounce) can coconut milk (unshaken)

2 ounces Red Curry Paste (page 154), or store-bought

1 pound boneless pork, cut into ½-inch thick slices

2 teaspoons fish sauce, or light soy sauce

2 teaspoons palm sugar, or brown sugar

½ cup bamboo shoots

1 tablespoon smooth unsalted peanut butter

1 cup fresh pineapple chunks

½ red bell pepper, thinly sliced

¼ cup Thai or sweet basil, roughly chopped

1. Preheat the electric pressure cooker by selecting sauté. When the inner pot is hot, after about 30 seconds, add 3 tablespoons of the thick cream from the top of the coconut milk can.

2. When it starts to bubble, stir in the curry paste and cook for a minute, until the mix thickens.

3. Stir in the remaining coconut milk and whisk until combined with the curry mix.

4. Add pork slices, fish sauce sugar, and bamboo shoots and give it a stir. Add peanut butter and gently push it down into the liquid, but do not stir. Turn off sauté.

5. Lock the lid in place. Select manual or pressure cook and adjust to high. Cook for 5 minutes on sealing mode.

6. When the cooking is complete, wait 5 minutes for natural pressure release, after which follow the quick-release method as per your cooker instructions. Unlock and remove the lid.

7. Turn on sauté mode. Add pineapple chunks and sliced red bell pepper. Simmer for 3 to 4 minutes.

8. Add the basil leaves and serve warm with steamed brown or white Jasmine Rice (page 158).

TIP: The combination of acidic and sweet flavors of pineapple makes it the perfect choice for this curry. Fresh pineapple chunks give the best results. If using canned pineapple instead, drain the juice and reduce the amount of palm sugar.

Thai Massaman Curry with Salmon // KAENG MASSAMAN

DAIRY-FREE • GLUTEN-FREE

Serves:
4

Prep Time:
15 minutes,
includes time
to prepare
curry paste

Cook Time:
4 minutes
(2 minutes
on sauté,
2 minutes on
low pressure)

Release:
Quick

Total Time:
30 minutes

Massaman curry is a relatively mild Thai red curry enriched by adding warming spices like cardamom, cinnamon, and cloves to the ingredients of a basic curry paste. Roasted peanuts, or in our case, peanut butter, add a nutty flavor and creamy texture to the curry. What sets this curry apart from most other Thai curries is the addition of Indian spices, which gives it an intense flavor.

1 (14-ounce) can coconut milk (unshaken)

2 ounces Red Curry Paste (page 154), or store-bought

¼ teaspoon ground cinnamon

½ teaspoon ground cardamom

⅛ teaspoon ground nutmeg

¼ teaspoon ground cloves

2 teaspoons fish sauce or soy sauce

1 to 2 teaspoons palm sugar or brown sugar

1 cup pumpkin or squash, cut into 1-inch chunks

1 pound salmon fillets (skinless), cut into 2-inch pieces

1 tablespoon smooth unsalted peanut butter

1 cup snow peas

2 tablespoons chopped cilantro leaves (for garnish)

1. Preheat the electric pressure cooker by selecting sauté. When the inner pot is hot, after about 30 seconds, add 3 tablespoons of the thick cream from the top of the coconut milk can.

2. When it starts to bubble, stir in the curry paste, cinnamon, cardamom, nutmeg, and cloves and cook for a minute, until the mix thickens.

3. Stir in the remaining coconut milk and whisk until combined with the curry mix.

4. Add the fish sauce, palm sugar, pumpkin chunks, and salmon pieces. Give it a stir. Add the peanut butter and gently push it down into the liquid, but do not stir. Turn off sauté.

5. Lock the lid in place. Select manual or pressure cook and adjust to low. Cook for 2 minutes on sealing mode.

6. When the cooking is complete, follow the quick-release method as per your cooker instructions to release the pressure. Unlock and remove the lid.

7. Stir in the snow peas and let the pot rest for 2 minutes. Garnish with cilantro leaves and serve with Coconut Rice (page 159).

TIP: Adding snow peas after pressure cooking retains their crunch. For a softer texture, add them along with the fish and pressure cook as per the instructions. To use store-bought Massaman Curry paste instead, add 2 to 3 ounces and skip the red curry paste and spices.

Beef Rendang
Curry // RENDANG DAGING

DAIRY-FREE • GLUTEN-FREE

Serves:
4

Prep Time:
15 minutes,
includes time
to prepare
curry paste

Cook Time:
43 minutes
(13 minutes
on sauté,
30 minutes
on high
pressure)

Release:
Quick

Total Time:
1 hour
8 minutes

Beef Rendang is a rich and spicy curry made in Indonesia, Malaysia, and Thailand. Unlike other curries, this is a "dry" curry, which means that the sauce is simmered down until there is just enough to coat the meat. This makes the end flavors more intense and robust. In this easy variation, we infuse the aroma and flavors of all the spices into the stew meat by pressure cooking and simmering the curry until the sauce reduces and the meat is fall-apart tender.

2 tablespoons coconut
or canola oil

1 pound beef stew meat cut
into 1-inch chunks

3 to 4 ounces Red Curry Paste
(page 154), or store-bought

2 tablespoons desiccated
coconut

¼ teaspoon ground cinnamon

½ teaspoon ground cardamom

¼ teaspoon ground cloves

¼ to ½ cup water (as needed)

1 cup coconut milk

1 teaspoon tamarind
concentrate

2 tablespoons dark soy sauce

2 teaspoons palm sugar
or brown sugar

2 tablespoons thinly sliced
scallions (for garnish)

1. Preheat the electric pressure cooker by selecting sauté and adjust to high. Wait for the pot to heat up, after about 30 seconds, and add the oil, beef cubes, curry paste, desiccated coconut, cinnamon, cardamom, and cloves and cook for 5 minutes, stirring 1 or 2 times in between.

2. Add water and scrape off any brown bits that may have stuck to the bottom. Add the coconut milk, tamarind concentrate, soy sauce, and sugar and stir. Turn off sauté.

3. Lock the lid in place. Select manual or pressure cook and adjust to high. Cook for 30 minutes on sealing mode.

4. When the cooking is complete, follow the quick-release method as per your cooker instructions. Unlock and remove the lid.

5. Select sauté and adjust to high. Check for seasoning and simmer for 6 to 8 minutes, until the sauce reduces down to your desired consistency.

6. Garnish with the sliced scallions and serve with Coconut Rice (page 159).

TIP: You can buy premade rendang curry paste in a can from the Asian aisle of large supermarkets or online. For this recipe, use 3 to 4 ounces of canned rendang paste (depending on spice preference) and skip the red curry paste, desiccated coconut, and dry spices.

Choo Chee Tofu Curry // CHOO CHEE

VEGAN • VEGETARIAN • DAIRY-FREE

Serves:
4 to 5

Prep Time:
15 minutes,
includes time
to prepare
curry paste

Cook Time:
3 minutes
(2 minutes
on sauté,
1 minute on
low pressure)

Release:
Quick

Total Time:
28 minutes

Choo Chee curry, also called Chu Chee, is a milder version of the traditional Thai red curry. The addition of toasted coconut to the curry base adds a rich and nutty flavor, which makes it ideal for cooking delicate foods like vegetables and seafood. In this recipe, we tweak red curry paste to make this mild and delicious curry using assorted vegetables and extra-firm tofu.

1 tablespoon coconut or canola oil

2 tablespoons desiccated coconut

1 (14-ounce) can coconut milk

1 teaspoon ground white pepper

2 ounces Red Curry Paste (page 154), or store-bought

1 tablespoon palm sugar, or brown sugar

2 teaspoons soy sauce

½ cup bamboo shoots

1 cup French green beans, halved

1 teaspoon freshly squeezed lime juice

½ teaspoon lime zest

1 cup sliced carrots

2 cups extra-firm tofu, cut into ½-inch pieces

¼ cup Thai or sweet basil leaves

1. Preheat the electric pressure cooker by selecting sauté. When the inner pot is hot, after about 30 seconds, add the oil and desiccated coconut. Stirring continuously, toast it for 30 to 40 seconds, until it begins to change color.

2. Stir in the coconut milk, white pepper, and curry paste. Cook for 1 minute until the mix combines well.

3. Add the sugar, soy sauce, bamboo shoots, green beans, lime juice, lime zest, carrots, and tofu and give them a stir. Turn off sauté.

4. Lock the lid in place. Select manual or pressure cook and adjust to low. Cook for 1 minute on sealing mode.

5. When the cooking is complete, follow the quick-release method as per your cooker instructions to release the pressure. Unlock and remove the lid.

6. Stir in the Thai basil and serve with steamed Jasmine Rice (page 158).

TIP: Fish is another popular choice for this curry. To make this curry with fish, simply substitute tofu with 1 pound of halibut, cod, mahi-mahi, or salmon cut into 2-inch chunks and cook for two minutes at low pressure, followed by a quick-release.

Jungle Curry // KAENG PA

VEGAN • VEGETARIAN • DAIRY-FREE • NUT-FREE

Serves:
4

Prep Time:
15 minutes,
includes time
to prepare
curry paste

Cook Time:
2 minutes
(1 minute
on sauté,
1 minute on
low pressure)

Release:
Quick

Total Time:
28 minutes

Jungle Curry, or Kaeng pa, is a red curry dish from the forests of northern Thailand. It is among the few curries that don't contain coconut milk since coconuts are not naturally found in that region. In the absence of the creamy coconut milk, the flavors of the curry paste are more pronounced. Like most other Thai curries though, a little sugar helps balance the heat from the chiles and brings the flavors together.

1 tablespoon coconut oil or canola oil

2 ounces Red Curry Paste (page 154), or store-bought

2 tablespoons soy sauce

¼ teaspoon dry ground ginger

½ teaspoon lime zest

1 teaspoon palm sugar or brown sugar

½ cup canned bamboo shoots

¾ cup canned baby corn

¾ cup sliced carrots

1 cup French beans, cut into 2-inch pieces

1 cup extra-firm tofu, cut into ½-inch cubes

1 cup zucchini, cut into 1-inch pieces

1 cup water

¼ cup Thai or sweet basil leaves

1. Preheat the electric pressure cooker by selecting sauté. When the inner pot is hot, after about 30 seconds, add the oil and curry paste. Cook for 1 minute, until fragrant.

2. Add the soy sauce, ginger, lime zest, sugar, bamboo shoots, corn, carrots, French beans, tofu, zucchini, and water and give it a stir. Turn off sauté.

3. Lock the lid in place. Select manual or pressure cook and adjust to low. Cook for 1 minute on sealing mode.

4. When the cooking is complete, use the quick-release method as per your cooker instructions. Unlock and remove the lid.

5. Stir in the Thai basil and serve with steamed Coconut Rice (page 159).

TIP: This curry is relatively spicy because it doesn't contain coconut milk, but it's very easy to customize to taste. For a milder curry, reduce the quantity of red curry paste to half. Alternatively, to make it spicier, stir in a tablespoon of store-bought chili-garlic paste or sriracha.

Japanese-Style Chicken Curry // KARE

DAIRY-FREE • NUT-FREE

Serves:
5

Prep Time:
10 minutes,
plus
10 minutes for
making roux

Cook Time:
17 minutes
(12 minutes
on sauté,
5 minutes on
high pressure)

Release:
Quick

Total Time:
38 minutes

Japan's famous dish Kare Raisu, meaning "curry rice," is a thick, mildly sweet curry made with meat chunks (chicken or beef), potatoes, onions, and carrots. Unlike other Asian curries that use palm sugar, the sweetness in this one comes from grated apple. It is probably the only curry in Asia that is made with a curry-spiced roux, which is essentially a flour and butter paste used to thicken sauces. Known for its signature brown sauce, this curry is one of the top comfort foods in Japan, along with ramen.

2 tablespoons canola oil

2 large onions, thinly sliced

1½ pounds boneless skinless chicken thighs, fat trimmed and halved

2 carrots, cut into 1-inch pieces

1 celery stalk, cut into ½-inch pieces

3 tablespoons butter

3 tablespoons all-purpose flour

½ teaspoon freshly ground black pepper

2 large gold potatoes, cut into 1-inch pieces

½ cup grated apple

1 teaspoon salt

2½ tablespoons curry powder

1½ cups water

Pinch salt

1 tablespoon tonkatsu sauce or Worcestershire sauce

1 tablespoon ketchup

1. Preheat the electric pressure cooker by selecting sauté. Adjust to high. When the inner pot is hot, after about 30 seconds, add the oil and onions with a pinch of salt. Stir and cook for 7 to 8 minutes, until the onions start browning.

2. Add the chicken and stir-fry for 2 minutes.

3. Add the carrots, celery, potatoes, apple, salt, 1½ tablespoons curry powder, and water. Give them a stir, scraping off any brown bits that may have stuck to the bottom, and turn off sauté.

4. Lock the lid in place. Select manual or pressure cook and adjust to high. Cook for 5 minutes on sealing mode.

5. While the curry is cooking, make the roux. Heat a skillet over medium heat. Melt the butter and whisk in the flour.

6. Keep stirring until the flour changes color to light brown. Stir in the remaining curry powder, black pepper, Tonkatsu sauce, and ketchup.

7. Turn off the heat and set the pan aside while you check on the curry.

8. When the cooking is complete, follow the quick-release method as per your cooker instructions to release the pressure. Unlock and remove the lid. Select sauté.

9. Add a couple of ladles of the hot curry into the roux and whisk until well combined and smooth.

10. Pour this mixture back into the curry pot while stirring gently. Simmer for 1 to 2 minutes until the curry thickens. Serve over Jasmine Rice (page 158).

TIP: You can opt for a store-bought Japanese curry paste in this recipe. Look for it in the Asian food aisle of your supermarket. To use that, follow steps 1-4 in this recipe, skip 5-7, then follow steps 8-10 using this curry paste.

Javanese-Style Chicken Curry // KARI AYAM

DAIRY-FREE • GLUTEN-FREE

Serves:
5

Prep Time:
15 minutes,
including
spice paste

Cook Time:
10 minutes
(5 minutes
on sauté,
5 minutes on
low pressure)

Release:
Natural
release for
5 minutes
followed by
quick

Total Time:
38 minutes

Kari Ayam is a coconut-milk-based chicken curry that originated in Java, Indonesia, but is equally popular in Malaysia. This nutty, spicy curry shares influences from Indian and Thai cuisine. This aromatic curry is reminiscent of an Indian korma made with nuts and coconut milk. In this recipe, we use a combination of curry powder and garam masala to create authentic kari ayam flavors.

FOR THE SPICE PASTE

2 tablespoons canola oil

½ cup roughly chopped shallots

1-inch fresh ginger, peeled

3 large garlic cloves

8 candlenuts or macadamia nuts

2 tablespoons lemongrass paste (or 1 teaspoon lime zest)

2 tablespoons curry powder

1 teaspoon Garam Masala (page 150)

1 tablespoon paprika

¼ teaspoon cayenne

2 to 3 tablespoons water

FOR THE CURRY

1½ pounds chicken breast or thighs, cut into 1-inch pieces

2 cups baby gold potatoes, halved

3 to 4 kaffir lime leaves or ½ teaspoon lime zest

1 teaspoon salt

1 teaspoon palm sugar or brown sugar

1 (14-ounce) can coconut milk

1. To make the spice paste, in a blender, combine the oil, shallots, ginger, garlic, nuts, lemongrass, curry powder, Garam Masala, paprika, and cayenne and grind to a smooth paste. If needed, add 2 to 3 tablespoons of water to blend.

2. Preheat the electric pressure cooker by selecting sauté. When the inner pot is hot, after about 30 seconds, add the spice paste and cook for 4 to 5 minutes stirring in between.

3. Stir in the chicken pieces, potatoes, lime leaves, salt, and sugar and cook for a minute. Stir in the coconut milk and turn off sauté. Scrape off any brown bits that may have stuck to the bottom.

4. Lock the lid in place. Select manual or pressure cook and adjust to low. Cook for 5 minutes on sealing mode.

5. When the cooking is complete, wait 5 minutes for natural pressure release, after which follow the quick-release method as per your cooker instructions. Unlock and remove the lid.

6. Serve hot over steamed Jasmine Rice (page 158).

TIP: This recipe calls for lemongrass paste. You can find it in the refrigerated produce section in large supermarkets in a reusable tube. Alternatively, you can use 1 teaspoon of lime zest.

Devil's Curry // KARI DEBAL

DAIRY-FREE • GLUTEN-FREE • NUT-FREE

Serves:
4 to 5

Prep Time:
10 minutes

Cook Time:
16 minutes
(10 minutes
on sauté,
6 minutes on
high pressure)

Release:
Natural
release for
10 minutes,
followed by
quick

Total Time:
46 minutes

Devil's Curry is a chicken dish made popular by the Portuguese Eurasian communities in Malacca, Malaysia. It is often served on special occasions, including Christmas. Also known as Kari Debal, this dish gets its flavors from a spice paste made of onion, ginger, garlic, lemongrass, and dried red chiles. In this easy adaptation, we use a combination of easily available ingredients, like paprika, cayenne, and vinegar, to create the same spicy and pungent flavors.

FOR THE SPICE PASTE

1 large onion chopped
in chunks

3 large garlic cloves

1-inch ginger, peeled

1 tablespoon paprika

½ teaspoon cayenne
(adjust to taste)

½ teaspoon turmeric

2 tablespoons lemongrass
paste or 1 teaspoon lime zest

1 tablespoon white vinegar

FOR THE CURRY

2 tablespoons canola oil

1 teaspoon mustard seeds

1½ pounds chicken thighs,
fat trimmed and halved

1 teaspoon salt

½ teaspoon sugar

2 large gold potatoes,
cut into 1-inch pieces

1½ cups water

½ head of cabbage cut
into 3 large segments

1. To make the spice paste, in a blender, combine the onion, garlic, ginger, paprika, cayenne, turmeric, lemongrass, and vinegar and blend to a smooth paste. If needed, add 2 to 3 tablespoons of water to blend.

2. Preheat the electric pressure cooker by selecting sauté. Adjust to high. When the inner pot is hot, after about 30 seconds, add the oil and mustard seeds.

3. When mustard seeds begin to splutter, add the spice paste. Sauté for 5 to 6 minutes until the paste turns darker in color.

4. Add the chicken pieces, salt, sugar, potatoes, and water. Give them a stir, scraping off any brown bits that may have stuck to the bottom, and turn off sauté.

5. Lock the lid in place. Select manual or pressure cook and adjust to high. Cook for 6 minutes on sealing mode.

6. When the cooking is complete, wait 10 minutes for natural pressure release, after which follow the quick-release method as per your cooker instructions. Unlock and remove the lid.

7. Select sauté. Check and adjust flavors to your taste. Add the cabbage and push it under the broth. Simmer for 4 to 5 minutes, until cabbage becomes soft, or until it reaches your desired tenderness. Turn off sauté.

8. Serve hot with steamed Basmati Rice (page 157).

TIP: This curry is known for its spicy flavors. You can easily customize it to suit your preference. For a milder curry, skip the cayenne. To make it spicier, double it.

Filipino-Style Beef Stew // MECHADO, MISTADO

DAIRY-FREE • NUT-FREE

Serves:
4

Prep Time:
10 minutes

Cook Time:
42 minutes
(12 minutes
on sauté,
30 minute on
high pressure)

Release:
Natural
release for
10 minutes,
followed by
quick

Total Time:
1 hour
12 minutes

Mechado, or Mistado, is a simple and hearty beef curry from the Philippines. Beef chunks, carrots, and potatoes are cooked in a tomato-based broth, seasoned with soy sauce and juice from a Filipino lime called Calamansi. In this recipe, we use the electric pressure cooker to cook the meat until it becomes fall-apart tender and the stew tastes like it has been simmering away for hours. Serve this Filipino comfort food with steamed Basmati Rice (page 157) or warmed bread rolls.

---

3 tablespoons canola oil
(1 tablespoon used first,
2 tablespoons used later)

½ red bell pepper, seeded
and cut into cubes

1 medium onion, finely
chopped

1 tablespoon minced garlic

1 pound beef stew meat, cut
into 1-inch chunks

¼ cup soy sauce

2 tablespoons tomato paste

½ cup crushed tomatoes
or 2 small Roma
tomatoes, puréed

2 medium gold potatoes,
peeled and quartered

1 large carrot, peeled and
cut into 2-inch cubes

1 teaspoon salt

1 teaspoon freshly cracked
black pepper

1 cup water

1 tablespoon freshly squeezed
lime juice (for finishing)

1. Turn on sauté. Adjust to high. Add 1 tablespoon of oil and wait for it to heat up. Add the bell peppers and sauté for 2 minutes. Remove and set aside for later.

2. Add the remaining 2 tablespoons of oil and the chopped onion. Sauté for 3 minutes.

3. Add the garlic and beef pieces and sauté another 3 minutes.

4. Add the soy sauce, tomato paste, crushed tomato, potatoes, carrot, salt, and pepper. Add water, give it a stir, and turn off sauté.

5. Lock the lid in place Select manual or pressure cook and adjust to high. Cook for 30 minutes on sealing mode.

6. When the cooking is complete, wait 10 minutes for natural pressure release, after which follow the quick-release method as per your cooker instructions. Unlock and remove the lid.

7. Select sauté and adjust to high. Stir in the fresh lime juice and sautéed peppers. Adjust the seasoning and simmer for 3 to 4 minutes until the curry thickens. Enjoy with steamed Jasmine Rice (page 158).

TIP: Calamansi lime tastes like a mix of orange and lime, more tart than sweet. It's not widely available here in the United States, but fresh lime juice works as a good substitute, especially since we're using only a tablespoon. However, you could add 1 teaspoon of orange juice to the curry if you wanted to mimic the taste of Calamansi limes.

Vegetable Coconut Curry // SAYUR LODEH

VEGETARIAN • DAIRY-FREE • GLUTEN-FREE

Serves:
5

Prep Time:
10 minutes

Cook Time:
5 minutes
(4 minutes
on sauté,
1 minute on
low pressure)

Release:
Quick

Total Time:
25 minutes

Sayur Lodeh is a popular vegetable stew from the island of Java. It is commonly served as part of a multicourse meal, especially during the Javanese communal feasts called Slametan. This curry is extremely versatile and can be customized with your preferred vegetables and can be transformed into an entrée by adding cubed firm tofu. It pairs great with Steamed Jasmine Rice (page 158) or with Indonesian rice cakes called Lontong.

FOR THE SPICE PASTE

1 tablespoon sambal oelek or chili-garlic sauce

1 large shallot, peeled and chopped

1 tablespoon lemongrass paste or 1 teaspoon lime zest

1-inch galangal or 1 tablespoon chopped ginger

1 tablespoon curry powder

½ teaspoon crushed red pepper flakes

10 candlenuts or macadamia nuts

2 to 3 tablespoons water (add more if needed)

FOR THE SAUCE

2 tablespoons vegetable oil

1 cup French beans, cut into 2-inch pieces

2 medium carrots, peeled and cut into 1-inch pieces

1 cup canned baby corn, drained

½ head cabbage, cut into large chunks

4 to 5 Thai green eggplant, quartered (see recipe tip for substitute)

1 (14-ounce) can coconut milk

¼ cup water

2 teaspoons palm sugar or brown sugar

½ teaspoon salt

1. To make the spice paste, in a blender, combine the sambal oelek, shallot, lemongrass paste, galangal, curry powder, red pepper, nuts, and water and blend until smooth.

2. Preheat the pressure cooker by selecting sauté. Wait for it to get hot, after about 30 seconds, and add the oil and the spice paste, and cook for 2 to 3 minutes, until fragrant.

3. Stir in the French beans, carrots, corn, cabbage, and eggplant and cook for a minute.

4. Add coconut milk, water, sugar, and salt and stir well. Turn off sauté.

5. Lock the lid into place. Select manual or pressure cook and adjust to low, then cook for 1 minute on sealing mode.

6. When the cooking is complete, release the pressure manually by following the quick-release method as per your cooker instructions. Unlock and remove the lid.

7. Check for seasoning and serve hot with steamed brown or white Jasmine Rice (page 158).

TIP: Thai eggplants are round, green vegetables, about 1½ to 2 inches in diameter. You can often find them in Asian supermarkets—for best results, look for bright green and firm eggplants. Alternatively, Indian purple eggplants (small) or Japanese eggplants cut into 1-inch chunks may be used in this dish.

Chinese-Style Chicken Curry

DAIRY-FREE • GLUTEN-FREE

Serves:
5

Prep Time:
10 minutes

Cook Time:
13 minutes
(8 minutes
on sauté,
5 minutes on
low pressure)

Release:
Natural
release for
5 minutes
followed by
quick

Total Time:
38 minutes

Although curry is not considered part of traditional Chinese cuisine, curry powder is added to a few dishes in southern China, where local food is influenced by Hong Kong–style fusion cuisine. In this simple and delicious curry, chicken and vegetables are cooked in coconut milk that is seasoned with Indian curry powder and Chinese five-spice blend. A touch of soy sauce ties it all together, and it is ready to be served in less time than it takes to order takeout.

2 tablespoons vegetable oil

1 pound boneless skinless chicken breast, cut into 1-inch chunks

2 teaspoons minced garlic

1 tablespoon minced ginger

1 medium onion, cut into small wedges

2 medium gold potatoes, cut into 1-inch pieces

1 tablespoon soy sauce

1 tablespoon Curry Powder, store-bought or homemade (page 151)

½ teaspoon Chinese five-spice powder

½ teaspoon cayenne

1 (14-ounce) can coconut milk, shaken

½ teaspoon sugar

½ teaspoon salt

1 cup frozen peas, thawed

1. Preheat the pressure cooker by selecting sauté. Adjust to high. Wait for it to get hot, about 30 seconds, and add the oil and chicken pieces and cook for 3 to 4 minutes.

2. Add the onion, garlic, and ginger and cook for another 2 minutes.

3. Turn off sauté. Add potatoes, soy sauce, curry powder, Chinese five-spice powder, cayenne, coconut milk, sugar, and salt and stir.

4. Lock the lid into place. Select manual or pressure cook and adjust to low, then cook for 5 minutes. When cooking is complete, release the pressure manually by following the quick-release method as per your cooker instructions. Unlock and remove the lid.

5. Select sauté and add the peas. Simmer for 2 to 3 minutes until the peas become soft.

6. Check for seasoning and serve hot with steamed brown or white Jasmine Rice (page 158).

TIP: Typically, the sauce in this dish has a thinner consistency. You can thicken it using a cornstarch slurry after pressure cooking. For the slurry, dissolve 2 teaspoons cornstarch in 3 tablespoons water. While the curry is simmering, stir in the slurry slowly. Let it simmer for another 2 to 3 minutes. The curry will thicken almost instantly with this method.

Cambodian-Style Chicken Curry // SOMLAR KARI SAEK MOUAN

DAIRY-FREE • GLUTEN-FREE

Serves:
5

Prep Time:
15 minutes,
includes time
to prepare
curry paste

Cook Time:
15 minutes
(5 minutes
on sauté,
10 minutes on
high pressure)

Release:
Natural
release for
10 minutes,
followed by
quick

Total Time:
50 minutes

This popular Cambodian Chicken Curry, also known as Somlar Kari Soek Mouan or Khmer Curry, is a perfect balance of sweet and spicy flavors and is influenced by neighboring Thai and Vietnamese cuisine. Traditionally, dried red chiles and fresh turmeric root are used to make the aromatic "kroeung" paste, which forms the base of this Cambodian specialty. In this recipe, we use a Thai red curry paste with ground turmeric as a convenient and easily available substitute.

2 tablespoons coconut or light olive oil

2 tablespoons Red Curry Paste (page 154), or store-bought

1 cup coconut milk

1½ pounds chicken drumsticks, skin removed

½ teaspoon ground turmeric

½ teaspoon salt

1 tablespoon fish sauce or soy sauce

2 teaspoons palm sugar or brown sugar

1 cup water

3 to 4 Thai or small Indian eggplant, cut into quarters

2 medium gold potatoes, cut into quarters

1. Preheat the pressure cooker by selecting sauté. Wait for it to get hot, after about 30 seconds, and add the oil and curry paste and cook for 2 minutes, until fragrant.

2. Add coconut milk and cook another 3 minutes. Turn off sauté.

3. Add the chicken drumsticks, turmeric, salt, fish sauce, sugar, water, eggplant, and potatoes and stir.

4. Lock the lid into place. Select manual or pressure cook and adjust to high, then cook for 10 minutes on sealing mode.

5. When the cooking is complete, wait 10 minutes for natural pressure release, after which follow the quick-release method as per your cooker instructions. Unlock and remove the lid.

6. Check for seasoning and adjust as needed. If you want to reduce the amount of sauce, select sauté and simmer for 3 to 4 minutes. Serve hot with steamed brown or white Jasmine Rice (page 158).

TIP: To use fresh turmeric root in this recipe, look for it in the refrigerated produce aisle, next to ginger. Peel and mince a ½-inch piece for this recipe and skip the turmeric powder. Make sure to wear food-grade gloves while handling fresh turmeric as it can stain your fingers.

Cambodian-Style Fish Curry // AMOK TREY

DAIRY-FREE • GLUTEN-FREE

Serves:
5

Prep Time:
15 minutes,
includes time
to prepare
curry paste

Cook Time:
4 minutes
(2 minutes
on sauté,
2 minutes on
low pressure)

Release:
Quick

Total Time:
30 minutes

Amok Trey, also known as "fish amok," translates to "steam-cooked fish" and is a traditional Cambodian curry. It is often prepared during the Water and Moon Festival held in late fall. In this traditional curry, fish pieces are coated with a mix of Cambodian spice paste called "kroeung" and coconut milk and is steamed in a banana leaf bowl. In this electric pressure cooker adaptation, we get the same sweet and spicy tender fish with a little extra sauce to enjoy with steamed rice.

1 tablespoon coconut or light olive oil

2 tablespoons Red Curry Paste (page 154), or store-bought

1 cup thick coconut milk

1 pound fish fillets (halibut, mahi-mahi or cod), cut into 2-inch pieces

½ teaspoon ground turmeric

½ teaspoon red pepper flakes

½ teaspoon salt

2 teaspoons fish sauce or soy sauce

1 teaspoon palm sugar or brown sugar

½ teaspoon Kaffir lime zest or regular lime zest

½ cup water

½ red bell pepper, julienned

½ cup Thai basil leaves

¼ cup cilantro leaves

1. Preheat the pressure cooker by selecting sauté. Wait for it to get hot, after about 30 seconds, and add the oil and curry paste and cook for 2 minutes, until fragrant. Turn off sauté.

2. Add the coconut milk and stir until it combines with the curry paste.

3. Add the fish, turmeric, red pepper flakes, salt, fish sauce, sugar, lime zest, water, bell pepper, Thai basil leaves, and cilantro and stir.

4. Lock the lid into place. Select manual or pressure cook and adjust to low, then cook for 2 minutes on sealing mode.

5. When the cooking is complete, follow the quick-release method as per your cooker instructions. Unlock and remove the lid.

6. Check for seasoning and serve hot with steamed brown or white Jasmine Rice (page 158).

TIP: Traditionally, this curry is a blend of sweet and spicy. You can, however, easily adjust the spice level to your taste. To make it mild, simply skip the red pepper flakes. To make it spicier, double the quantity.

JUNGLE CURRY, PAGE 74

HARISSA EGGPLANT & CHICKPEAS, PAGE 104

CHAPTER 4

MIDDLE EAST & AFRICA

When we think of Middle Eastern cuisine, we tend to think of *Doner Kebab*, *Gyros*, *Baba Ghanoush*, and other grilled dishes. But this region has some of the most unique curries.

Popular meat curries from this part of the globe are made with lamb, chicken, or beef, which are often cooked with locally grown fruits and nuts, like dates, pomegranate, figs, pistachio, and walnuts. A classic example would be the Persian stew called *Fesenjan*, in which the meat is cooked with pomegranate molasses and toasted ground walnuts.

Curries in North Africa have a Mediterranean and Middle Eastern influence, with spices like saffron and cinnamon added to the basic curry seasoning. Slow-cooked meat dishes like *Tagine*, which are essentially thick curries with intense flavors and aroma, are popular in Morocco and Tunisia.

East African curries consist of lentils and vegetables in addition to meat dishes and are very similar in cooking style to Indian curries. Good examples would be popular Ethiopian stews like Doro Wat *(Chicken Curry)* and Alicha Wot *(Split Peas Curry)*. This region also has a few nut-based curries, like *Kunde*, in which a simple black-eyed pea curry is thickened with roasted ground peanuts.

Durban Curry

GLUTEN-FREE • NUT-FREE

Serves:
5

Prep Time:
10 minutes

Cook Time:
15 minutes
(5 minutes
on sauté,
10 minutes on
high pressure)

Release:
Natural
release for
10 minutes,
followed by
quick

Total time:
45 minutes

Durban Curry is a spicy and robust dish that comes from the city of Durban in South Arica, which has the largest concentration of Indian population in Africa. It is a fiery red curry that gets its heat from cayenne peppers and is balanced by the subtle sweet flavors of cinnamon and fennel. Durban Curry is usually served over rice, with condiments like pickle, chutney, and sambal, or you can ladle it in a hollowed-out bread bowl and enjoy the famous Bunny Chow.

2 tablespoons ghee or butter

1 teaspoon cumin seeds

1 medium onion, finely chopped

8 to 10 curry leaves

1 tablespoon minced ginger

1 tablespoon minced garlic

1½ pounds chicken drumsticks, skin removed

1 cup canned diced tomatoes or 2 Roma tomatoes chopped

1 teaspoon salt

1 tablespoon Garam Masala (page 150)

1 tablespoon ground coriander

2 teaspoons ground cumin

½ to ¾ teaspoon cayenne pepper (adjust to taste)

¼ teaspoon ground cinnamon

½ teaspoon ground fennel

2 potatoes cut into 1-inch cubes

1 cup water

2 tablespoons fresh cilantro, chopped

1. Preheat the electric pressure cooker by selecting sauté. When the inner pot is hot, about 30 seconds, add the ghee and cumin seeds.

2. When the cumin seeds begin to sizzle, add the onion, curry leaves, ginger, and garlic and cook for 3 minutes, till the onions soften.

3. Add the chicken, tomatoes, salt, garam masala, coriander, cumin, cayenne, cinnamon, and fennel. Cook for 2 to 3 minutes till the tomatoes soften and break down. Turn off sauté. Add potatoes and water and stir.

4. Lock the lid in place. Select manual or pressure cook and adjust to high. Cook for 10 minutes on sealing mode.

5. When the cooking is complete, wait 10 minutes for natural pressure release, after which follow the quick-release method as per your cooker instructions. Unlock and remove the lid.

6. Stir in the cilantro and serve with steamed Basmati Rice (page 157) or in a bread bowl.

TIP: To make this curry mild, use 2 teaspoons of regular paprika instead of cayenne pepper. For Bunny Chow, hollow out a bread bowl and ladle the curry in for serving.

Cape Malay Chicken Curry

DAIRY-FREE • GLUTEN-FREE • NUT-FREE

Serves:
5

Prep Time:
15 minutes

Cook Time:
13 minutes
(7 minutes
on sauté,
6 minutes on
high pressure)

Release:
Natural
release for
10 minutes,
followed by
quick

Total Time:
48 minutes

Here's an easy weeknight recipe for a traditional Cape Malay Chicken Curry, a perfect blend of sweet and sour flavors. Cape Malay is a fusion cuisine that comes from people of India, Malaysia, and Indonesia who were brought to Cape Town during the colonial period. They adapted recipes by incorporating local fruits with traditional cooking techniques and unique spices blends. This curry is one of those classics!

2 tablespoons olive oil

1 medium onion, finely chopped

1 jalapeño, seeded, ribs removed, and finely diced

2 teaspoons minced garlic

1½ tablespoons minced ginger

1½ pounds boneless skinless chicken thighs, fat trimmed and cut into 2-inch pieces

1 tablespoon Garam Masala (page 150)

2 tablespoons ground coriander

1 teaspoon ground cumin

½ teaspoon ground turmeric

¼ teaspoon ground cinnamon

1 teaspoon ground fennel seeds

½ teaspoon ground cardamom

1 teaspoon red pepper flakes (adjust to taste)

1 teaspoon salt

3 medium gold potatoes, cut into 1-inch chunks

1 large carrot, peeled and cut into medallions

3 to 4 Roma tomatoes pureed

2 tablespoons smooth apricot jam

1 cup water

Light squeeze of lemon juice

2 tablespoons fresh cilantro, chopped (for garnish)

1. Preheat the electric pressure cooker by selecting sauté and adjust to high. When the inner pot is hot, about 30 seconds, add the olive oil, onion, jalapeño, garlic, and ginger. sauté for 4 to 5 minutes, until the onions turn translucent.

2. Add the chicken pieces, Garam Masala, coriander, cumin, turmeric, cinnamon, fennel, cardamom, red pepper flakes, and salt. Stir and cook for another 2 minutes.

3. Add the potatoes, carrot, tomato, apricot jam, and water. Stir well and cancel sauté.

4. Lock the lid in place. Select manual or pressure cook and adjust to high. Cook for 6 minutes on sealing mode.

5. When the cooking is complete, wait 10 minutes for natural pressure release, after which follow the quick-release method as per your cooker instructions. Unlock and remove the lid.

6. Squeeze a few drops of lemon juice, garnish with cilantro and serve over steamed Basmati Rice (page 157).

TIP: Apricot jam enhances the traditional sweet-tart fruity flavor to this curry. For an alternative without refined sugar, you can soak 10 dried apricots in hot water and puree them with the tomatoes.

Beef Tagine

DAIRY-FREE • GLUTEN-FREE • NUT-FREE

Serves:
4

Prep Time:
10 minutes

Cook Time:
38 minutes
(8 minutes
on sauté,
30 minutes
on high
pressure)

Release:
Natural
release for
10 minutes,
followed by
quick

Total Time:
1 hour
8 minutes

In Morocco, an everyday meat and potatoes stew is cooked in a ceramic or clay vessel called a tagine, which traps the heat and steam cooks the food. It is one of the most iconic dishes from that region. A classic tagine is made with meat, vegetables, and dried fruit and is seasoned with warm spice blend, called *ras el hanout*. In this recipe, we use an electric pressure cooker to mimic the cooking style of a tagine and give our curry a slow-cooked flavor in much less time than a traditional recipe.

FOR THE RAS EL HANOUT SPICE MIX

1 tablespoon coriander powder

2 teaspoons paprika

1 teaspoon cumin powder

1 teaspoon ground ginger

½ teaspoon turmeric

½ teaspoon black pepper

½ teaspoon cardamom

¼ teaspoon ground cinnamon

¼ teaspoon ground cloves

FOR THE SAUCE

2 tablespoons oil

1 medium onion, chopped

1 pound beef stew meat, cut into 1-inch chunks

1 cup crushed tomatoes or 2 tablespoons tomato paste

1 cup water

4 medium gold potatoes, peeled and halved

6 to 8 prunes or dates, chopped
(see Tip for substitute)

1 cup frozen peas, thawed

1. To make the *ras el hanout* spice mix, in a small bowl, mix together the coriander, paprika, cumin, ginger, turmeric, black pepper, cardamom, cinnamon, and cloves and set aside.

2. Preheat the electric pressure cooker by selecting sauté. When the inner pot is hot, about 30 seconds, add the oil and onion. Cook for 2 minutes.

3. Add the beef chunks and *ras el hanout* spice mix and sauté for 3 to 4 minutes. Turn off sauté.

4. Add the crushed tomatoes and water and scrape off any brown bits that may have stuck to the bottom. Add the potatoes and prunes or dates and give them a stir.

5. Lock the lid in place. Select manual or pressure cook and adjust to high. Cook for 30 minutes on sealing mode.

6. When the cooking is complete, wait 10 minutes for natural pressure release, after which follow the quick-release method as per your cooker instructions. Unlock and remove the lid.

7. Select sauté and add the thawed peas. Simmer for 2 to 3 minutes until the peas soften. Adjust the seasoning and serve with Buttered Couscous (page 164).

TIP: In Moroccan cuisine, dried fruits are commonly used to add a subtle sweet flavor to the curry. If you don't have dried fruits on hand, 1 to 2 teaspoons of preserves like plum jam or date spread make a good substitute. Alternatively, you can add 1 to 2 teaspoons of honey.

Moroccan-Style Lamb Curry

DAIRY-FREE • GLUTEN-FREE • NUT-FREE

Serves:
6

Prep Time:
10 minutes

Cook Time:
30 minutes
(10 minutes
on sauté,
20 minutes
on high
pressure)

Release:
Natural
release for
10 minutes,
followed by
quick

Total time:
1 hour

Moroccan lamb curry is a traditional dish made by slow-cooking boneless lamb in a tomato broth that is infused with an aromatic spice blend called *ras el hanout*. Unique ingredients such as lemon peel and dried apricots add aroma and a subtle sweetness, making this one of the top comfort foods from this region. In this recipe, we use a quick to assemble homemade *ras el hanout* spice blend and lemon zest to create the same flavors.

FOR THE RAS EL HANOUT SPICE MIX

1 tablespoon coriander powder

2 teaspoons paprika

1 teaspoon cumin powder

1 teaspoon ground ginger

½ teaspoon turmeric

½ teaspoon black pepper

½ teaspoon cardamom

¼ teaspoon ground cinnamon

¼ teaspoon ground cloves

FOR THE SAUCE

3 tablespoons olive oil

1 bay leaf

1 medium onion, finely chopped

1 tablespoon minced garlic

2 pounds boneless lamb shoulder, cut into 2-inch pieces

2 cups crushed tomatoes, or 3 large Roma tomatoes, pureed

1¼ teaspoons salt (adjust to taste)

3 tablespoons ras el hanout spice mix

¼ cup dried apricots, quartered

Zest of 1 lemon

1 large carrot, cut into ½-inch discs

1½ cups diced sweet potato

1 cup water

2 tablespoons chopped parsley (for garnish)

1. To make *ras el hanout* spice mix, in a small bowl, mix together the coriander, paprika, cumin, ginger, turmeric, black pepper, cardamom, cinnamon, and cloves and set aside.

2. Preheat the electric pressure cooker by selecting sauté. When the inner pot is hot, about 30 seconds, add the olive oil, bay leaf, onion, and garlic. Cook for 4 to 5 minutes, until the onions become translucent.

3. Add the lamb pieces, tomatoes, salt, and *ras el hanout* spice mix. Sauté for 2 to 3 minutes.

4. Add in the apricots, lemon zest, carrot, sweet potato, and water and stir, scraping off any brown bits that may have stuck to the bottom. Turn off sauté.

5. Lock the lid in place. Select manual or pressure cook and adjust to high. Cook for 20 minutes on sealing mode.

6. When the cooking is complete, wait 10 minutes for natural pressure release, after which follow the quick-release method as per your cooker instructions. Unlock and remove the lid.

7. Select sauté and simmer for 2 to 3 minutes, until the curry thickens.

8. Garnish with parsley and serve with Buttered Couscous (page 164).

TIP: Traditionally, preserved lemons are used in this curry. You can buy them in the international food aisle of large stores or online. If using these, take 1 preserved lemon, rinse and finely chop it, and add it to this recipe instead of lemon zest.

Harissa Eggplant & Chickpeas

VEGAN • VEGETARIAN • DAIRY-FREE • GLUTEN-FREE

Serves:
5

Prep Time:
10 minutes

Cook Time:
10 minutes
(5 minutes
on sauté,
5 minutes on
high pressure)

Release:
Quick

Total time:
30 minutes

Harissa is a North African spice paste made by blending assorted red chilies, garlic, olive oil, and dry spices such as coriander, cumin, and caraway seeds, and some recipes include sun-dried tomatoes as well. In this naturally vegan and gluten-free dish, a short 5-minute pressure cooking cycle helps infuse the sweet and spicy flavors of harissa into the eggplant and chickpeas beautifully.

2 tablespoons extra virgin olive oil

1 large eggplant, peeled and cut into 1-inch cubes

1 medium onion, sliced thin

1 red bell pepper, sliced

¼ to ½ cup water (as needed)

1 cup crushed tomato, or 2 medium Roma tomatoes, pureed

1 (14-ounce) can chickpeas, rinsed and drained

2 to 3 tablespoons Harissa Paste (page 153), or store-bought

¾ teaspoon salt (adjust to taste)

1 teaspoon coriander powder

½ teaspoon turmeric

Squeeze of lemon

2 tablespoons chopped fresh parsley

1. Preheat the electric pressure cooker by selecting sauté. When the inner pot is hot, about 30 seconds, add the oil, eggplant, onions, and bell peppers. Cook 4 to 5 minutes, stirring in between.

2. Add the water to scrape off any brown bits that may have stuck to the bottom of the pot. Then add the tomatoes, chickpeas, Harissa paste, salt, coriander, and turmeric, and stir well. Turn off sauté,

3. Lock the lid in place. Select manual or pressure cook and adjust to high. Cook for 5 minutes on sealing mode.

4. When the cooking is complete, follow the quick-release method as per your cooker instructions to release the pressure. Unlock and remove the lid.

5. If you want to reduce the amount of sauce, sauté and simmer for 2 to 3 minutes. Add lemon juice and parsley. Serve as a side dish or entrée with Buttered Couscous (page 164).

TIP: To further enhance this dish and add a subtle smoky flavor, replace the fresh red bell pepper with jarred roasted red peppers. Drain one pepper, slice it, and add to the pot as per instructions.

Spicy Chicken Curry // DORO WAT

DAIRY-FREE • GLUTEN-FREE • NUT-FREE

Serves:
4

Prep Time:
10 minutes,
includes time
to prepare
Berbere
Seasoning

Cook Time:
14 minutes
(8 minutes
on sauté,
6 minutes on
high pressure)

Release:
Natural
release for
5 minutes
followed by
quick

Total Time:
40 minutes

There's a good reason why this spicy Ethiopian chicken stew is the national dish of Ethiopia. In this traditional curry, chicken is cooked with a classic onion-tomato gravy, seasoned liberally with the fiery Berbere spice mix, and topped with hard-boiled eggs before serving. The electric pressure cooker does a fantastic job of infusing all the earthy flavors of the spices in the sauce and chicken in less than an hour.

3 tablespoons ghee or unsalted butter

1 large onion, finely chopped

1 tablespoon minced ginger

1 tablespoon minced garlic

2 tablespoons Berbere spice mix (page 152), or store-bought

2 tablespoons tomato paste

1 cup water, divided

1½ pounds boneless skinless chicken thighs, fat trimmed and halved

4 hard-boiled eggs, shelled

2 tablespoons chopped cilantro (for garnish)

1. Preheat the electric pressure cooker by selecting sauté. Adjust to high. When the inner pot is hot, about 30 seconds, add the ghee. Add the onions with a pinch of salt and cook for 7 to 8 minutes, until they start browning.

2. Add the ginger and garlic, and sauté another minute.

3. Add the Berbere spice mix, tomato paste, and ¼ cup water and stir well. Turn off sauté.

4. Add the remaining water and scrape off any brown bits that may have stuck to the bottom. Add the chicken and stir.

5. Lock the lid in place. Select manual or pressure cook and adjust to high. Cook for 6 minutes on sealing mode.

6. In the meantime, boil the eggs (see Tip to make them in the same pot). Once the eggs have cooled enough to handle, peel them. Using a fork, pierce them all over to allow them to soak the sauce.

7. When the cooking is complete, wait 5 minutes for natural pressure release, after which follow the quick-release method as per your cooker instructions. Unlock and remove the lid.

8. Cut the hard-boiled eggs in half and add them to the curry. Garnish with cilantro and serve with steamed Basmati Rice (page 157).

TIP: To make this a one-pot dish, you can cook the eggs along with the chicken curry using the pot-in-pot cooking method. To do that, assemble the curry as per directions. Place a 3- to 4-inch metal trivet or stand in the pot. Place the eggs on top of that and close the lid. Pressure cook as per directions. After cooking, remove eggs and place them in ice-cold water for 5 minutes. Peel and slice the eggs in half.

Split Peas Curry // ALICHA WOT

VEGETARIAN • DAIRY-FREE • GLUTEN-FREE

Serves:
4

Prep Time:
10 minutes

Cook Time:
12 minutes
(4 minutes
on sauté,
8 minutes on
high pressure)

Release:
Natural
release for
10 minutes,
followed by
quick

Total time:
42 minutes

Alicha Wot is a mild Ethiopian stew in which split peas are cooked with onions, ginger, and turmeric in seasoned clarified butter called Niter-Kibbeh. "Wot" in Ethiopian means "stew" and "Alicha" refers to a mild style of cooking. In my easy take on this simple and satisfying curry, I infuse store-bought clarified butter (or ghee) with an Ethiopian spice blend called Berbere to achieve similar results, and these creamy split peas come together in less than an hour.

2 tablespoons ghee or butter

2 to 3 teaspoons Berbere spice mix (page 152), or store-bought

½ onion, finely chopped

2 teaspoons minced garlic

½ tablespoon minced ginger

¾ cup yellow split peas, rinsed and drained

½ teaspoon turmeric

2 cups water

1. Select sauté and adjust to medium. Add the ghee and Berbere spice mix. Stir to combine. Heat the mix till it starts bubbling.

2. Add the onion, garlic, and ginger and cook for 4 to 5 minutes, until the onions turn translucent.

3. Add the rinsed split peas, turmeric, and water. Give it a stir and turn off sauté.

4. Lock the lid in place. Select manual or pressure cook and adjust to high. Cook for 8 minutes on sealing mode. For a softer texture, increase the time to 10 minutes.

5. When the cooking is complete, wait 10 minutes for natural pressure release, after which follow the quick-release method as per your cooker instructions. Unlock and remove the lid.

6. Using a potato masher or the back of a cooking spoon, mash the lentils till they reach a creamy texture. Serve warm with Buttered Couscous (page 164) or sourdough bread.

TIP: If you can find Niter Kibbeh (seasoned clarified butter), use 2 tablespoons in this recipe instead of ghee. Note about Berbere: Store-bought Berbere blends tend to vary in taste, so start by adding 1 teaspoon and add more later after tasting the curry.

Fish Coconut Curry // MTUZI WA SAMAKI

DAIRY-FREE • GLUTEN-FREE

Serves:
4

Prep Time:
10 minutes

Cook Time:
9 minutes
(7 minutes
on sauté,
2 minutes on
low pressure)

Release:
Quick

Total Time:
28 minutes

Tanzanian Fish Curry, natively called "Mtuzi wa Samaki" is a traditional Swahili fish curry cooked across East Africa. This curry originated in city of Zanzibar and is now enjoyed all over the eastern coast of Africa. In this mildly spiced dish, fish is cooked in a flavorful sauce made with coconut milk and tomatoes and is seasoned with curry powder. Peanuts enrich the curry and give it a smooth, creamy flavor. Here is an easy recipe using peanut butter as a convenient replacement.

FOR THE MARINADE

1½ pounds fish fillets, cut into 2-inch pieces (halibut, mahi-mahi or cod)

½ teaspoon salt

½ teaspoon turmeric

Juice of ½ lemon

FOR THE SAUCE

2 tablespoons coconut oil or canola oil

1 medium onion, finely chopped

1 tablespoon minced garlic

2 teaspoons minced ginger

1 (14-ounce) can diced tomatoes, or 3 to 4 Roma tomatoes

2 tablespoons curry powder

½ teaspoon freshly crushed black pepper

2 teaspoons paprika

¼ teaspoon cayenne powder

½ teaspoon salt (adjust to taste)

¼ cup water (or as needed)

½ green bell pepper, chopped in 1-inch pieces

1 cup coconut milk

1 tablespoon smooth unsalted peanut butter

Squeeze of lemon

2 tablespoons chopped cilantro

1. Toss the fish with the salt, turmeric, and lemon juice and set aside while you prepare other ingredients and start the sauce.

2. For the sauce, preheat the electric pressure cooker by selecting sauté. When the inner pot is hot, about 30 seconds, put in the oil, onion, garlic, and ginger. Cook for 4 to 5 minutes, until onions turn translucent.

3. Add the tomato , curry powder, black pepper, paprika, cayenne, and salt. Stir and cook for 2 minutes, until the tomatoes start breaking down. Turn off sauté.

4. Add the water and scrape off any brown bits that may have stuck to the bottom of the pot. Then add the green pepper, fish, and coconut milk, and stir. Add the peanut butter and gently push it into the liquid, but do not stir.

5. Lock the lid in place. Select manual or pressure cook and adjust to low. Cook for 2 minutes on sealing mode.

6. When the cooking is complete, follow the quick-release method as per your cooker instructions to release the pressure. Unlock and remove the lid.

7. Squeeze in about a teaspoon of fresh lemon juice. Stir in the chopped cilantro and serve with steamed Basmati Rice (page 157).

TIP: You can use other kinds of proteins in this recipe instead of fish. For chicken, cut into 1-inch pieces and adjust the cooking time to 5 minutes followed by a natural pressure release. For a vegetarian version, replace fish with extra-firm tofu cut into ½-inch cubes and follow the same cooking time and instructions.

Coconut Chicken Curry // KUKU PAKA

DAIRY-FREE • GLUTEN-FREE • NUT-FREE

Serves:
5

Prep Time:
10 minutes

Cook Time:
10 minutes
(6 minutes
on sauté,
4 minutes on
high pressure)

Release:
Natural
release for
5 minutes
followed by
quick

Total Time:
35 minutes

Kuku Paka, also called "kuku na nazi," is a chicken dish with a coconut-based curry that originates from the East African coast. With a heavy influence from Indian cuisine, it is very popular among the Indian communities living in Kenya, Tanzania, and Uganda. Traditionally, the chicken is char-grilled before adding to the coconut curry, which gives it a smoky flavor. In my easy take on this traditional recipe, we add smoked paprika to achieve a similar earthy-smoky taste.

1 tablespoon ghee
or unsalted butter

1 medium onion, finely
chopped

½ green bell pepper, diced

1 jalapeño, seeded and sliced

1 tablespoon minced garlic

1 tablespoon minced ginger

1½ pounds chicken breast,
cut into bite-size pieces

1 tablespoon Curry Powder
or garam masala

1 teaspoon smoked paprika

1 teaspoon salt

½ teaspoon turmeric

1 tablespoon tomato paste
or ½ cup crushed tomatoes

1 (14-ounce) can coconut milk

2 teaspoons fresh lemon juice

2 tablespoons chopped fresh
cilantro (for garnish)

1. Preheat the electric pressure cooker by selecting sauté. When the inner pot is hot, about 30 seconds, add the ghee, onion, pepper, garlic, and ginger and cook for 4 to 5 minutes, stirring 2 or 3 times in between.

2. Add the chicken pieces, curry powder, paprika, salt, and turmeric and cook for another 2 minutes.

3. Add the tomato paste and coconut milk and stir. Turn off sauté.

4. Lock the lid in place. Select manual or pressure cook and adjust to high. Cook for 4 minutes on sealing mode.

5. When the cooking is complete, wait 5 minutes for natural pressure release, after which follow the quick-release method as per your cooker instructions. Unlock and remove the lid.

6. Stir in the lemon juice and check for seasoning. Garnish with cilantro and serve with steamed Basmati Rice (page 157).

TIP: A popular variation of this curry is served with hard-boiled eggs. To do that, simply hard-boil 4 large eggs. Once the eggs have cooled enough to handle, peel them. Using a fork, pierce them all over, to allow them to soak the sauce. Cut them in half and place them in the curry, cut-side facing up.

Black-Eyed Peas Curry // KUNDE

VEGETARIAN • DAIRY-FREE • GLUTEN-FREE

Serves:
5

Prep Time:
10 minutes

Cook Time:
10 minutes
(5 minutes
on sauté,
5 minutes on
high pressure)

Release:
Natural
release for
5 minutes
followed by
quick

Total Time:
35 minutes

I n Kenya, this creamy stew is a popular way to cook Kunde, Swahili for "black-eyed peas." In this traditional recipe, roasted peanuts (ground or paste) are used to flavor a simple curry made with onions and tomato, and chopped greens are often added to stretch the dish. It is mildly seasoned with salt and pepper, so the peanut flavor really shines in the end, adding a rich taste and texture. It is commonly served over steamed rice or a traditional side called "Ugali."

2 tablespoons oil

1 medium onion, finely chopped

1 cup diced canned tomato or 2 to 3 Roma tomatoes

1 teaspoon salt

1 teaspoon freshly ground black pepper

2 (14-ounce) cans black-eyed peas, rinsed and drained

2 cups chopped baby spinach or kale

1½ cups water

¼ cup smooth unsalted peanut butter

1. Preheat the electric pressure cooker by selecting sauté. When the inner pot is hot, about 30 seconds, add the oil and onion and cook for 2 to 3 minutes, until the onions soften.

2. Add the tomatoes, salt, and pepper and cook another 2 minutes, until the tomatoes break down. Add the black-eyed peas, spinach, and water and give it a stir. Add the peanut butter and gently push it under the liquid without stirring. Turn off sauté.

3. Lock the lid in place. Select manual or pressure cook and adjust to high. Cook for 5 minutes on sealing mode.

4. When the cooking is complete, wait 5 minutes for natural pressure release, after which follow the quick-release method as per your cooker instructions. Unlock and remove the lid.

5. Stir to mix the peanut butter in the curry. Serve with steamed Basmati Rice (page 157).

TIP: If using dried black-eyed peas, rinse and drain them. Add them to the recipe as per instructions and pressure cook at high for 15 minutes, followed by a natural pressure release. Follow the remaining instructions and enjoy these creamy peas in less than an hour.

Lamb in Yogurt Sauce // MANSAF

GLUTEN-FREE

Serves:
5

Prep Time:
10 minutes

Cook Time:
30 minutes
(10 minutes
on sauté,
20 minutes
on high
pressure)

Release:
Natural
release for
10 minutes,
followed by
quick

Total Time:
1 hour

Mansaf is a traditional Middle Eastern dish in which lamb is cooked in a sauce made of fermented dried yogurt (Jameed) and served with rice over a thin flatbread. This curry is the national dish of Jordan and is also eaten in Palestine, Iraq, Israel, Southern Syria, and Saudi Arabia. Since Jameed is found in select few international food stores, I substitute it with thick Greek yogurt here and achieve a similar creamy and tangy taste in this recipe.

3 tablespoons ghee or
unsalted butter, divided

2 tablespoons slivered
almonds (for garnish)

2 tablespoons pine nuts
(for garnish)

2 bay leaves

1½ pounds boneless lamb leg
or shoulder cut into
2-inch pieces

1 large onion, finely chopped

1 tablespoon minced garlic

1 tablespoon cumin powder

2 teaspoons coriander powder

1 teaspoon freshly ground
black pepper

1 teaspoon cardamom powder

1 teaspoon salt (adjust
to taste)

¼ teaspoon ground cloves

¼ teaspoon ground cinnamon

⅛ teaspoon ground nutmeg

¼ teaspoon saffron

2 cups plain Greek or thick
yogurt (divided)

½ cup water

1 tablespoon cornstarch

2 tablespoons chopped
mint leaves

1. To prepare the garnish, preheat the electric pressure cooker by selecting sauté. When the inner pot is hot, about 30 seconds, add 1 tablespoon ghee along with the almonds and pine nuts. Stir and cook for about 45 seconds. Remove promptly to prevent the nuts from burning. Reserve for garnish.

2. Add the remaining ghee with the bay leaves, lamb pieces, and chopped onion. Cook for 4 to 5 minutes, stirring 2 or 3 times in between.

3. Add the garlic, cumin, coriander, black pepper, cardamom, salt, cloves, cinnamon, nutmeg, and saffron and sauté the lamb for another minute.

4. Whisk 1 cup of yogurt until smooth. Add it and the water to the pot, and water and scrape off any brown bits that may have stuck to the bottom of the pot. Turn off sauté.

5. Lock the lid in place. Select manual or pressure cook and adjust to high. Cook for 20 minutes on sealing mode.

6. When the cooking is complete, wait 10 minutes for natural pressure release, after which follow the quick-release method as per your cooker instructions. Unlock and remove the lid.

7. Select sauté to thicken the curry. While the curry is simmering, mix the cornstarch into the remaining 1 cup of yogurt. Add a ladle of curry into the yogurt and mix to temper it. Pour the yogurt mix back in the pot while stirring continuously.

8. Simmer the sauce for 4 to 5 minutes till it thickens. Check for seasoning and turn off sauté.

9. Top with toasted almonds, pine nuts, and mint and serve with steamed Basmati Rice (page 157).

TIP: Greek or thick yogurt is key to making a creamy curry in this recipe. If using regular yogurt instead, use 2 cups of full-fat yogurt with ½ teaspoon of sugar to balance out the extra tang.

Pomegranate Chicken Curry // FESENJAN

DAIRY-FREE • GLUTEN-FREE

Serves:
5

Prep Time:
20 minutes,
includes time
to toast and
grind walnuts.

Cook Time:
20 minutes
(10 minutes
on sauté,
10 minutes on
high pressure)

Release:
Natural
release for
10 minutes,
followed by
quick

Total Time:
1 hour

Khoresh-e Fesenjān, or simply Fesenjān, is a Persian curry that is often served at Shab-e-Yalda, an Iranian holiday to celebrate the longest night of the year and the beginning of winter. In this rich curry, the chicken is browned and cooked with sweet and tangy pomegranate syrup and ground toasted walnuts. The result is a luxurious sweet, tart, and thick curry that is served over steamed rice.

1½ cups walnut halves

3 tablespoons olive oil

1 large onion, finely chopped

2 teaspoons minced garlic

1½ pounds chicken drumsticks, skin removed

1 teaspoon salt

½ teaspoon freshly ground black pepper

¼ teaspoon ground cinnamon

½ teaspoon saffron

2 cups water

¼ cup pomegranate molasses (see Tip for substitute)

2 tablespoons brown sugar (adjust to taste)

1. To toast the walnuts, spread them on a microwave-safe plate and heat in 2-minute increments for 4 to 5 minutes. Cool completely. Using a spice or coffee grinder, grind them to a fine powder. Set aside for later.

2. Preheat the electric pressure cooker by selecting sauté. When the inner pot is hot, about 30 seconds, add the oil and onion and cook for 5 minutes, stirring 2 or 3 times in between.

3. Add the garlic, chicken drumsticks, salt, black pepper, cinnamon, and saffron. Stir and cook for 4 to 5 minutes.

4. Add the water and scrape off any brown bits that may have stuck to the bottom. Turn off sauté. Add the pomegranate molasses and ground walnuts and push them under the liquid but do not stir.

5. Lock the lid in place. Select manual or pressure cook and adjust to high. Cook for 10 minutes on sealing mode.

6. When the cooking is complete, wait 10 minutes for natural pressure release, after which follow the quick-release method as per your cooker instructions. Unlock and remove the lid.

7. Stir to combine walnuts and add sugar to taste. Serve with steamed Basmati Rice (page 157).

TIP: Pomegranate molasses adds a unique sweet-tart flavor to the curry. It is available in all Middle Eastern grocery stores. You can substitute it with 1 cup of cranberry or pomegranate concentrated juice (not cocktail) and reduce the water to 1 cup. You may need to add an extra tablespoon of sugar to balance the flavors.

COCONUT CHICKEN CURRY, PAGE 112

CARIBBEAN FISH CURRY, PAGE 128

CHAPTER 5

THE CARIBBEAN & LATIN AMERICA

n the 1800s, the British enlisted more than a million laborers from the Indian subcontinent for their cane and rubber plantations throughout Mauritius, Fiji, South Africa, Guyana, and the Caribbean. These migrants brought their curry recipes with them and morphed them into new dishes incorporating local ingredients like fruits, nuts, and produce.

Everyday dishes in most Caribbean islands include some combination of rice, plantains, beans, cassava (a root vegetable), culantro (an herb similar to cilantro), bell peppers, chickpeas, tomatoes, sweet potatoes, and coconut. A popular herb and oil paste, called green seasoning, is used as a base for many curries and stews, and curry powder is used as a primary spice blend.

Latin America, on the other hand, is a highly diverse area and its cuisine shares cultural influences with Africa, Europe, Native America, and Asia. Rice and beans are a staple in most countries around here. Curries like Cuban-Style Black Beans (page 136) and Red Bean Curry (page 144) are part of everyday meals in Cuba, Puerto Rico, and surrounding countries.

An aromatic paste called *Sofrito* forms the base for most curries in Latin American cuisine. The actual recipe may vary by region, but it is typically made of onions, garlic, peppers, and cilantro. *Sazón* and *adobo* are the two main seasoning blends used to flavor meat and bean dishes.

In this chapter, you'll find quick recipes for commonly used seasonings and sauces in addition to a variety of curries from the Caribbean and Latin American kitchens.

Caribbean Curried Chicken

DAIRY-FREE • GLUTEN-FREE • NUT-FREE

Serves:
5

Prep Time:
10 minutes

Cook Time:
14 minutes
(8 minutes
on sauté,
6 minutes on
high pressure)

Release:
Natural
release for
10 minutes,
followed by
quick

Total Time:
44 minutes

Caribbean Curried Chicken is one of the most popular recipes from Jamaica and the surrounding region. Although there are many variations of this chicken and potato curry, most use an aromatic herb and chili paste called "green seasoning" as the base for this dish. The sauce is seasoned with Jamaican curry powder, which is essentially Indian curry powder mixed with ground fenugreek seeds and allspice.

FOR THE GREEN SEASONING

1 large onion, cut into chunks

3 garlic cloves

1 Scotch bonnet or habanero pepper, seeded

3 sprigs thyme (leaves only) or ½ teaspoon dried thyme

2 scallions

1 cup cilantro

1 cup parsley

FOR THE CURRY

2 tablespoons coconut oil or canola oil

1½ pounds boneless skinless chicken thighs, fat trimmed and halved

2½ tablespoons Jamaican curry powder (see Tip for substitute)

1 teaspoon salt

1 cup diced potatoes

1 cup water

Juice of ½ lime or lemon

1. To make the green seasoning, in a food processor or blender, combine the onion, garlic, pepper, thyme, scallion, cilantro, and parsley and blend to a fine consistency.

2. Preheat the electric pressure cooker by selecting sauté. When the inner pot is hot, after about 30 seconds, add the oil and the green seasoning. Cook for 5 minutes, stirring 2 or 3 times.

3. Add the chicken, Jamaican curry powder, and salt and cook another 2 to 3 minutes. Turn off sauté.

4. Add the potatoes and water and give it a stir. Scrape off any brown bits that may have stuck to the bottom.

5. Lock the lid in place. Select manual or pressure cook and adjust to high. Cook for 6 minutes on sealing mode.

6. When the cooking is complete, wait 10 minutes for natural pressure release, after which follow the quick-release method as per your cooker instructions. Unlock and remove the lid.

7. Add fresh lime juice and check for seasoning. Enjoy with steamed Basmati Rice (page 157).

TIP: Jamaican curry powder is available in specialty food markets and online. If you cannot find it, you can use 1½ tablespoon of Curry Powder (page 151) plus ½ teaspoon of allspice powder.

Jamaican-Style Curried Goat

DAIRY-FREE • GLUTEN-FREE • NUT-FREE

Serves:
4

Prep Time:
10 minutes

Cook Time:
35 minutes
(5 minutes
on sauté,
30 minutes
on high
pressure)

Release:
Natural
release for
10 minutes,
followed by
quick

Total Time:
1 hour
5 minutes

Jamaican-style Curried Goat is made by slow-cooking goat stew meat with potatoes in a tomato-based sauce seasoned with spicy curry powder. The heat in this curry comes from the fiery Scotch bonnet peppers, also known as Caribbean peppers. A little goes a long way with these peppers, so we just use one in this recipe. The final dish is a delicious spicy curry with fall-apart tender meat and creamy potatoes. And like most meat curries, it tastes even better the next day.

1 large onion, finely chopped

1 tablespoon minced garlic

1 tablespoon minced ginger

1 Scotch bonnet or habanero pepper, seeded

2 scallions, white part only

2 tablespoons coconut oil or canola oil

1 pound bone-in goat stew meat

1 teaspoon salt

3 tablespoons Jamaican curry powder (see Tip on page 125 for substitute)

½ teaspoon dried thyme

1 cup diced potatoes

1 cup crushed tomatoes or ¼ cup tomato paste

1 cup water

Reserved green stalk of scallions, thinly sliced (for garnish)

1. In a mini food processor or blender, put the onion, garlic, ginger, Scotch bonnet pepper, and scallion. Pulse 8 to 10 times, until everything is finely chopped.

2. Preheat the electric pressure cooker by selecting sauté. When the inner pot is hot, after about 30 seconds, add the oil and the chopped aromatics from step 1. Cook for 2 minutes.

3. Add the goat meat, salt, curry powder, and thyme and sauté for 3 minutes. Add potatoes, tomatoes, and water and stir well. Scrape off any brown bits that may have stuck to the bottom. Turn off sauté.

4. Lock the lid in place. Select manual or pressure cook and adjust to high Cook for 30 minutes on sealing mode.

5. When the cooking is complete, wait 10 minutes for natural pressure release, after which follow the quick-release method as per your cooker instructions. Unlock and remove the lid.

6. Check for seasoning, garnish with reserved sliced scallions, and enjoy with Coconut Rice (page 159).

TIP: Goat meat can be found in most halal meat shops. To make this curry with lamb instead, use 1 pound of boneless lamb leg or shoulder cut into 2-inch pieces. Follow the recipe and adjust cooking time to 20 minutes followed by a natural pressure release.

Caribbean Fish Curry

DAIRY-FREE • GLUTEN-FREE • NUT-FREE

Serves:
4

Prep Time:
10 minutes

Cook Time:
7 minutes
(5 minutes
on sauté,
2 minutes on
low pressure)

Release:
Quick

Total Time:
27 minutes

Caribbean Fish Curry is a zesty dish with a kick. Tender fillets of fish are cooked in a creamy coconut milk sauce, seasoned with spicy Scotch bonnet pepper and curry powder. Crushed tomatoes add acidity and give this dish a gorgeous orange hue. Here's an easy pressure cooker recipe in which fish soaks up flavors of the Caribbean in less than 30 minutes. This mild family-friendly curry can be easily made with shrimp or chicken instead.

1 pound snapper or salmon fish fillet cut into 2-inch pieces

1 teaspoon salt

2½ tablespoons Curry Powder (page 151) (½ tablespoon used first, 2 tablespoons used later)

½ teaspoon dried thyme

1 medium onion, chopped finely

1 teaspoon minced garlic

1 teaspoon minced ginger

1 Scotch bonnet or habanero pepper, seeded

1 scallion, chopped

2 tablespoons coconut or canola oil

½ teaspoon allspice powder

1 cup crushed tomatoes or 2 Roma tomatoes puréed

¼ cup water (or as needed)

½ red bell pepper, diced

1 cup coconut milk

1 to 3 drops of fresh lemon juice

2 tablespoons chopped parsley (for garnish)

1. Season the fish with the salt, ½ tablespoon curry powder, and thyme and refrigerate while you prepare other ingredients.

2. In a food processor or chopper, put the onion, garlic, ginger, Scotch bonnet pepper, and scallion. Pulse a few times until finely chopped.

3. Preheat the electric pressure cooker by selecting sauté. When the inner pot is hot, after about 30 seconds, add the chopped aromatic mixture from the previous step and cook for 3 minutes.

4. Add the remaining curry powder, allspice powder, and tomatoes and cook for 2 minutes, until the tomatoes break down. Turn off sauté. Add the water and stir, scraping off any brown bits that may have stuck to the bottom.

5. Add the seasoned fish, bell pepper, and coconut milk and stir well.

6. Lock the lid in place. Select manual or pressure cook and adjust to low pressure. Cook for 2 minutes on sealing mode.

7. When the cooking is complete, follow the quick-release method as per your cooker instructions to release the pressure. Unlock and remove the lid.

8. Add the lemon juice and adjust seasoning. Garnish with parsley and serve with Coconut Rice (page 159).

TIP: Snapper is the most common choice for this curry since it holds its shape and absorbs the curry flavors really well. Other firm white fish, such as tilapia, cod, catfish, sea bass, mahi-mahi, and haddock, would also work well in this recipe.

Mexican-Style Pulled Pork // COCHINITA PIBIL

DAIRY-FREE • GLUTEN-FREE

Serves:
8

Prep Time:
10 minutes

Cook Time:
40 minutes
on high

Release:
Natural
release for
15 minutes
followed by
quick

Total Time:
1 hour
15 minutes

Cochinita Pibil is a Yucatan-style barbecue pork in which the meat is marinated with citrus juices and a chili paste called achiote, made of annatto seeds, which gives this dish a deep red color and earthy flavor. Traditionally, the marinated meat is wrapped in banana leaves and slow-cooked in an underground smoker known as a pib. In this simple recipe, we use store-bought achiote paste and pressure-cook the pork until it is fall-apart tender.

FOR THE SPICE PASTE

1¾ to 2 ounces achiote paste

4 garlic cloves

1 tablespoon paprika

2 teaspoons oregano

2 teaspoons cumin

1 cup freshly squeezed
orange juice

2 tablespoons lime juice
or apple cider vinegar

1½ teaspoons salt

1 teaspoon freshly cracked
black pepper

FOR THE PORK

3 pounds pork shoulder or
loin, cut into 1-inch chunks

½ to 1 cup water

1. To make the spice paste, in a food processor, put in the anchiote paste, garlic, paprika, oregano, cumin, orange juice, lime juice, salt, and black pepper and blend to a smooth paste.

2. Add the pork pieces in the cooking pot of your electric pressure cooker and pour this spice paste on top. Toss to combine.

3. Add the water and lock the lid in place. Select manual or pressure cook and adjust to high. Cook for 40 minutes on sealing mode.

4. When the cooking is complete, wait 15 minutes for natural pressure release, after which follow the quick-release method as per your cooker instructions. Unlock and remove the lid.

5. Put the pork pieces in a wide bowl. Using two forks, shred the meat. Pour a few ladles of the seasoned liquid from the pressure cooker, until the meat is moist (not soaked).

6. Serve with a side of pickled red onions and enjoy on tacos or with Spanish Rice (page 161).

TIP: Traditionally, Cochinita Pibil is served with a side of pickled onions. You can purchase a store-bought version or make your own. To do so, in a microwave-safe bowl, combine ½ cup of apple cider vinegar, 2 teaspoons of sugar, ¾ teaspoon of salt, and ¼ teaspoon of cayenne (optional). Microwave for 1 minute or until the mix is hot. Thinly slice one large red onion and toss it in the vinegar mix. Cover and set aside to marinate.

Chicken Mole // MOLE POBLANO

DAIRY-FREE • GLUTEN-FREE • NUT-FREE

Serves:
4

Prep Time:
10 minutes

Cook Time:
13 minutes
(5 minutes
on Saute,
8 minutes on
high pressure)

Release:
Natural
release for
10 minutes,
followed by
quick

Total Time:
45 minutes

Chicken Mole is a unique sweet and spicy tomato and chocolate sauce from the state of Pueblo and Oaxaca in Mexico. In a classic Mole Poblano sauce, chile peppers and tomatoes are simmered together with raisins, pumpkin seeds, and chocolate, and then cooked chicken is added to it. In our easy pressure cooker variation, we cook the sauce and chicken in the same pot, and in less than an hour, we have juicy, tender chicken soaked in authentic Mole sauce.

2 tablespoons oil

1 medium onion, chopped in chunks

¼ cup pepitas (see Tip for substitute)

3 garlic cloves, chopped

2 tablespoons Mexican chili powder

2 tablespoons raisins or agave syrup

½ cup freshly squeezed orange juice

¼ teaspoon ground cinnamon

2 tablespoons unsweetened cocoa powder

2 chipotle chiles in adobo sauce plus 1 tablespoon more of the adobo sauce

1 (14-ounce) can fire-roasted diced tomatoes

2 pounds chicken breast

2 tablespoons chopped cilantro (for garnish)

1. Preheat the electric pressure cooker by selecting sauté. When the inner pot is hot, after about 30 seconds, put in the oil and onion and cook for 3 minutes to soften them.

2. Add the pepita seeds and garlic and cook another 2 minutes.

3. Stir in the Mexican chili powder, raisins, orange juice, cinnamon, cocoa powder, chipotle chiles, additional adobo sauce, and tomatoes. Turn off sauté. Place the chicken in the sauce.

4. Lock the lid in place. Select manual or pressure cook and adjust to high pressure. Cook for 8 minutes on sealing mode.

5. When the cooking is complete, wait 10 minutes for natural pressure release, after which follow the quick-release method as per your cooker instructions. Unlock and remove the lid.

6. Put the chicken on a plate. Using two forks, shred it.

7. Using an immersion blender, purée the sauce to a smooth paste. If using a traditional blender, wait for the sauce to cool down before blending. Add the shredded chicken back into the sauce and stir.

8. Garnish with cilantro and serve on corn tortillas or with Spanish Rice (page 161).

TIP: Pepitas, or pumpkin seeds, can be found in most supermarkets. However, if you cannot find them, you can substitute slivered almonds.

Chipotle Shrimp Curry

DAIRY-FREE • GLUTEN-FREE • NUT-FREE

Serves:
5

Prep Time:
10 minutes

Cook Time:
8 minutes
(5 minutes
on sauté,
3 minutes on
low pressure)

Release:
Quick

Total Time:
28 minutes

Chipotle Shrimp Curry is a smoky and mildly spicy curry that'll satisfy your Mexican takeout cravings. The base of this bold and intense sauce is fire-roasted tomatoes and chipotle chiles that are marinated in adobo sauce. In this weeknight-friendly recipe, we take a few convenient shortcuts and use canned fire-roasted tomatoes and chipotle chiles and achieve restaurant-quality flavors in a little over 30 minutes.

1 medium onion, finely chopped

2 teaspoons minced garlic

2 tablespoons canola oil

1 cup fire-roasted tomatoes, diced or crushed

3 chipotle chiles in adobo sauce plus 1 tablespoon sauce

1 teaspoon Mexican chili powder

2 teaspoons cumin powder

1 tablespoon paprika

½ teaspoon freshly crushed black pepper

1 teaspoon salt

1 tablespoon red wine vinegar or apple cider vinegar

½ cup water (add more as needed)

1 pound shrimp, extra-large (21 to 30 count per pound), peeled and deveined

2 teaspoons honey or agave syrup

3 tablespoons chopped cilantro (for garnish)

1. In a food processor, pulse the onion chunks and garlic, until finely chopped. Alternatively, finely chop by hand.

2. Preheat the electric pressure cooker by selecting sauté. When the inner pot is hot, after about 30 seconds, add the oil, onions, and garlic, and cook for 3 minutes to soften them.

3. Add the tomatoes, chiles, chili powder, cumin, paprika, black pepper, salt, and vinegar and cook for 2 minutes, until the tomatoes break down. Turn off sauté. Add the water and scrape off any brown bits that may have stuck. Add the shrimp.

4. Lock the lid in place. Select manual or pressure cook and adjust to low. Cook for 3 minutes on sealing mode.

5. When the cooking is complete, follow the quick-release method as per your cooker instructions to release the pressure. Unlock and remove the lid.

6. Stir in the honey and check for seasoning. Garnish with cilantro and serve with Spanish Rice (page 161).

TIP: As a variation, add 1 cup of sliced bell peppers along with the onions and serve this dish with warmed corn tortillas and enjoy chipotle shrimp tacos. Add smaller shrimp after pressure cooking and simmer on sauté mode until cooked through and opaque, about 3 to 5 minutes.

Cuban-Style Black Beans // FRIJOLES NEGRO

VEGAN • DAIRY-FREE • GLUTEN-FREE • NUT-FREE

Serves:
6

Prep Time:
10 minutes

Cook Time:
8 minutes
(3 minutes
on sauté,
5 minutes on
high pressure)

Release:
Natural
release for
5 minutes
followed by
quick

Total Time:
33 minutes

"Frijoles Negros" means "black beans" in Spanish. It is a staple dish in Cuba, Venezuela, Mexico, and other nations in Latin America. In this simple yet satisfying dish, black beans are seasoned with cumin, oregano, and vinegar. Make it with dried or canned black beans—either way, you will enjoy the creamiest and tastiest Cuban Black Beans in less than an hour.

1 medium onion, chopped in chunks

½ green pepper, chopped in chunks

3 garlic cloves

2 tablespoons canola oil

1 bay leaf

2 (15-ounce) cans of black beans, drained (see Tip for using dried black beans)

2 teaspoons cumin powder

2 teaspoons dried oregano

¾ teaspoon salt (adjust to taste)

2 teaspoons red wine vinegar or apple cider vinegar

1 cup water

3 tablespoons chopped fresh cilantro (for garnish)

1. In a mini food processor, pulse the onion, pepper, and garlic until finely chopped. Alternatively, finely chop by hand.

2. Preheat the electric pressure cooker by selecting sauté. When the inner pot is hot, after about 30 seconds, add the oil, bay leaf, onions, green pepper, and garlic and cook for 3 minutes to soften them.

3. Add the drained black beans, cumin, oregano, salt, and vinegar. Add the water and stir well. Turn off sauté.

4. Lock the lid in place. Select manual or pressure cook and adjust to high. Cook for 5 minutes on sealing mode.

5. When the cooking is complete, wait 5 minutes for natural pressure release, after which follow the quick-release method as per your cooker instructions. Unlock and remove the lid.

6. Select sauté and simmer the beans for 2 to 3 minutes to reduce the sauce. Using the back of a spoon or ladle, mash a few beans to thicken the curry.

7. Garnish with cilantro and serve with Spanish Rice (page 161).

TIP: To make this curry with dried black beans, rinse 1 cup of dried beans and soak them in 3 cups of water overnight or for 8 hours. Before cooking, drain and rinse them. Follow the recipe and pressure cook for 25 minutes at high pressure, followed by a natural pressure release.

Beef Picadillo

DAIRY-FREE • GLUTEN-FREE • NUT-FREE

Serves:
4

Prep Time:
10 minutes

Cook Time:
12 minutes
(2 minutes
on sauté,
10 minutes on
high pressure)

Release:
Natural
release for
10 minutes,
followed by
quick

Total Time:
42 minutes

Cuban Beef Picadillo is a traditional hash-like stew made with ground beef, tomatoes, raisins, potatoes, and green olives. It's a perfect blend of flavors, with the raisins adding a subtle sweetness to counter the saltiness from the pimento-stuffed olives. It is popular in many Latin American countries, so the ingredients may vary by region. Picadillo is often served with rice or used as a filling for tacos or a stuffing in savory pastries.

2 tablespoons canola oil

1 bay leaf

1 pound ground beef

1 medium onion,
finely chopped

3 to 4 garlic cloves, minced

½ red bell pepper,
finely chopped

3 medium potatoes cut into
½-inch cubes

1 tablespoon red wine vinegar
(or apple cider vinegar)

1 (14.5-ounce) can diced
tomatoes

1 teaspoon salt

½ teaspoon freshly crushed
black pepper

1 teaspoon dried oregano

1 tablespoon ground cumin

2 teaspoons paprika

¼ teaspoon cayenne powder

½ cup green olives with
pimentos

½ cup raisins

½ cup water (as needed)

1. Preheat the electric pressure cooker by selecting sauté. When the inner pot is hot, after about 30 seconds, put in the oil, bay leaf, and ground beef. Cook for 5 minutes, stirring in between. Using a ladle, break up any lumps of ground beef.

2. Add the onion, garlic, and bell pepper and cook for another 2 minutes.

3. Add the potatoes, vinegar, tomatoes, salt, pepper, oregano, cumin, paprika, cayenne, olives, raisins, and water and stir. Add more water as needed, and scrape off any brown bits that have stuck to the bottom. Turn off sauté.

4. Lock the lid in place. Select manual or pressure cook and adjust to high. Cook for 10 minutes on sealing mode.

5. When the cooking is complete, wait 10 minutes for natural pressure release, after which follow the quick-release method as per your cooker instructions. Unlock and remove the lid. If you want to reduce the sauce further, select Saute and simmer for 2 to 3 minutes until it reaches your desired consistency.

6. Serve warm with Spanish Rice (page 161), or with warmed tortillas.

TIP: Some popular variations of this recipe also include capers. To add those, drain ¼ cup of capers and either add whole or coarsely chopped, along with the olives.

Brazilian Fish Stew // MOQUECA

DAIRY-FREE • GLUTEN-FREE • NUT-FREE

Serves:
4

Prep Time:
10 minutes

Cook Time:
7 minutes
(5 minutes
on sauté,
2 minutes on
low pressure)

Release:
Quick

Total Time:
27 minutes

Moqueca is a mild fish stew from the coastal state of Espirito Santo in eastern Brazil. It is made with firm white fish, onions, bell peppers, tomatoes, cilantro, lime, and coconut milk, and seasoned lightly with black pepper and red pepper flakes. Traditionally, it is slow-cooked in a terracotta pot with fish or a mix of prawns and fish. Slow-cooking allows the fish to absorb the curry flavors while holding its shape. In this recipe, we accomplish the same flavor and texture by cooking it under low pressure.

1 pound of halibut (or sword-fish or cod) fillets, cut into 2-inch pieces

1 tablespoon minced garlic

¾ teaspoon salt

½ teaspoon freshly ground black pepper

2 tablespoons freshly squeezed lime juice or lemon juice

2 tablespoons olive oil

1 medium onion, sliced

1 red or yellow bell pepper, sliced

1 (14.5-ounce) can diced tomatoes or 2 to 3 fresh tomatoes chopped

2 scallions, thinly sliced

6 tablespoons chopped cilantro (4 tablespoons used first, 2 tablespoons for garnish

1 tablespoon paprika

½ teaspoon red pepper flakes

1 cup packed cilantro leaves

1 (14-ounce) can coconut milk

1. Season the fish with garlic, salt, pepper, and lime juice. Set aside while you prepare the sauce.

2. Preheat the electric pressure cooker by selecting sauté. When the inner pot is hot, after about 30 seconds, put in the oil, onion, and bell pepper, and cook for 3 minutes, until softened.

3. Add the tomatoes, scallions, 4 tablespoons of cilantro, paprika, and red pepper flakes. Cook for another 2 to 3 minutes until the tomatoes soften.

4. Add the cilantro leaves and coconut milk and stir. Turn off sauté.

5. Lock the lid in place. Select manual or pressure cook and adjust to low. Cook for 2 minutes on sealing mode.

6. When the cooking is complete, follow the quick-release method as per your cooker instructions to release the pressure. Unlock and remove the lid.

7. Check for seasoning and add more lime juice if needed. Garnish with cilantro and serve with steamed Basmati rice (page 157).

TIP: A popular variation of *Moqueca*, called *Capixaba*, is made without coconut milk. To make that, follow this recipe and add 1 cup of chicken stock instead of coconut milk.

Puerto Rican-Style Chicken Curry // POLLO GUISADO

DAIRY-FREE • GLUTEN-FREE • NUT-FREE

Serves:
6

Prep Time:
10 minutes

Cook Time:
16 minutes
(6 minutes
on sauté,
10 minutes on
high pressure)

Release:
Natural
release for
10 minutes,
followed by
quick

Total Time:
46 minutes

Pollo Guisado is a braised chicken stew from the islands of Puerto Rico, Cuba, and Dominican Republic. A pesto-like paste of onion, garlic, bell pepper, and cilantro called sofrito forms the flavor base of this stew, which is seasoned liberally with a flavorful Latin American spice blend called sazón. In this recipe, we use homemade sofrito and store-bought sazón to create an authentic Puerto Rican chicken and potato curry.

1 medium onion, chopped in chunks

½ green bell pepper, chopped in chunks

3 garlic cloves

¼ cup packed cilantro

2 tablespoons olive oil

1 bay leaf

2 pounds chicken drumsticks, skin removed

3 to 4 tablespoons sazón

3 tablespoons tomato paste

2 medium carrots, sliced

3 medium gold potatoes, cut into 1-inch cubes

½ cup pimento-stuffed green olives

1 cup water

1. To make the sofrito, in a food processor or blender, put in the onion, bell pepper, garlic, and cilantro. Blend until finely minced.

2. Preheat the electric pressure cooker by selecting sauté. When the inner pot is hot, after about 30 seconds, put in the oil and bay leaf. Add the sofrito and cook for 5 minutes, stirring in between.

3. Add the chicken drumsticks, sazón, and tomato paste. Sauté for 1 minute.

4. Add the carrots, potato, olives, and water and stir. Scrape off any brown bits stuck to the bottom. Turn off sauté.

5. Lock the lid in place. Select manual or pressure cook and adjust to high. Cook for 10 minutes on sealing mode.

6. When the cooking is complete, wait 10 minutes for natural pressure release, after which follow the quick-release method as per your cooker instructions. Unlock and remove the lid.

7. Adjust the seasoning and serve with steamed Basmati Rice (page 157).

TIP: If you're having trouble finding sazón seasoning, fear not—you can make your own! Just mix together the following ingredients: 2 teaspoons of ground coriander, 2 teaspoons of ground cumin, 2 teaspoons of dried oregano, 2 teaspoons of paprika, 1 teaspoon of salt, ½ teaspoon of ground black pepper, ½ teaspoon of garlic powder, and ½ teaspoon of turmeric powder.

Red Bean Curry // HABICHUELAS GUISADAS

VEGAN • VEGETARIAN • DAIRY-FREE • GLUTEN-FREE

Serves:
5

Prep Time:
10 minutes

Cook Time:
11 minutes
(6 minutes
on sauté,
5 minutes on
high pressure)

Release:
Natural
release for
5 minutes
followed by
quick

Total Time:
36 minutes

Stewed beans, called Habichuelas Guisadas, are a staple in most Puerto Rican meals. These flavorful beans are simmered in a tomato-and-sofrito-based broth, along with potatoes and manzanilla olives. Traditionally, dried red beans are soaked and simmered until beans cook through and all the flavors blend well. In our quick-and-easy adaptation, we use canned kidney beans to make this comforting and creamy bean curry.

1 medium onion, chopped in chunks

½ green bell pepper, chopped in chunks

3 garlic cloves

¼ cup packed cilantro, plus an additional 2 tablespoons (for garnish)

2 tablespoons olive oil

1 bay leaf

1 cup crushed tomatoes or 2 Roma tomatoes, puréed

3 to 4 tablespoons sazón

2 (15-ounce) cans kidney beans, drained and rinsed

1 medium carrot, chopped

3 medium gold potatoes or pumpkin, cut into 1-inch cubes

¼ cup pimento-stuffed green olives

1 cup water

1. To make sofrito, in a food processor, put in the onion, bell pepper, garlic, and ¼ cup of cilantro and blend until finely minced.

2. Preheat the electric pressure cooker by selecting sauté. When the inner pot is hot, after about 30 seconds, put in the oil and bay leaf. Add the sofrito and cook for 4 to 5 minutes, stirring in between.

3. Add the tomatoes and sazón. Sauté for 1 minute.

4. Add the beans, carrot, potatoes, olives, and water and stir. Turn off sauté.

5. Lock the lid in place. Select manual or pressure cook and adjust to high. Cook for 5 minutes on sealing mode.

6. When the cooking is complete, let the pressure release naturally, after which unlock and remove the lid.

7. Garnish with remaining chopped cilantro and serve with steamed Basmati Rice (page 157).

TIP: You can make this recipe with dried red or kidney beans as well. Rinse and soak 1 cup of dried beans in 3 cups of water, overnight or for at least 8 hours. Add as per recipe directions and pressure cook for 35 minutes at high pressure, followed by a natural pressure release.

MEXICAN-STYLE PULLED PORK, PAGE 130

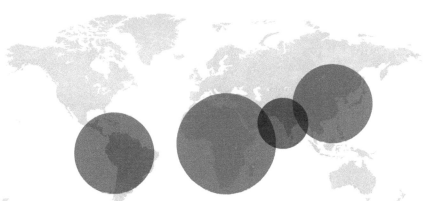

CHAPTER 6

SPICE MIXES & OTHER STAPLES

The difference between a "good" and an "amazing" curry depends largely on the spices used to flavor it. What you pair it with, whether rice or flatbread, also makes a big difference. This chapter is dedicated to the flavor-building spice blends and popular sides that enhance curries around the world.

Making a spice blend or paste from scratch may seem time-consuming or intimidating, but most of these can be made in 10 to 15 minutes with easily accessible ingredients. And thanks to online shopping, ethnic spices are now available to most people. Freshly made spice blends add a vibrant touch to any recipe.

In this chapter, I have included recipes for popular spice blends like garam masala, curry powder, thai curry paste, and berbere, to name just a few. There are many variations of these spice blends, as the ingredients differ according to region and individual preferences, but I have chosen the most commonly used ones.

Most of these dry spice blends stay fresh for a few months. Just store them in an airtight container in a dark, cool place. Similarly, curry pastes can be made in advance and stored in the refrigerator or freezer to extend their life. Whenever I'm making Thai curry pastes, I double or triple the recipe and store the excess in small mason jars or ice-cube trays.

This chapter also features popular staples like roti and couscous that are enjoyed with curry, with rice being the common starch among most cultures.

Garam Masala

VEGAN • VEGETARIAN • DAIRY-FREE • GLUTEN-FREE • NUT-FREE

Makes:
¼ cup

Cook Time:
2 minutes

Total Time:
13 minutes

G aram Masala is a fragrant blend of ground spices commonly used in Indian cuisine. The word "garam" means "hot" and refers to the warming spices used in this blend, and "masala" means "spices." Typically, the spices are toasted to bring out the flavor, and then ground to a fine consistency. Here's a classic Punjabi-style recipe that has been in my family for four generations.

3 tablespoons coriander seeds

1 tablespoon cumin seeds

2 teaspoons green cardamom seeds

1 teaspoon whole cloves

1 teaspoon whole black peppercorns

2-inch flat cinnamon bark

2 dried bay leaves

1. Lightly toast the coriander, cumin, cardamom, cloves, black peppercorns, cinnamon, and bay leaves for 2 minutes over medium heat in a dry skillet, until fragrant. Stir often.

2. Turn off the heat and transfer to a plate to stop the cooking. Cool for 10 minutes.

3. Transfer to a spice or coffee grinder and grind to a fine powder. Store in an airtight container.

TIP: Another popular variation includes fennel, nutmeg, and black cardamom seeds. For that, simply add 1 teaspoon of fennel seeds and 1 black cardamom pod while toasting, then stir in a ½ teaspoon of freshly grated nutmeg to the final blend.

Curry Powder

VEGAN • VEGETARIAN • DAIRY-FREE • GLUTEN-FREE • NUT-FREE

Makes:
¼ cup

Prep Time:
2 minutes

Total Time:
2 minutes

Curry Powder is a variation of the Indian garam masala that was popularized by the British in the 1800s. Contrary to popular belief, it is not used in Indian cooking. The British created curry powder as a milder seasoning for Indian curries, after which the powder crossed boundaries with trade and colonization. Used in many Asian, African, and Caribbean dishes, most curry powder recipes include coriander, cumin, mustard, and chile peppers in addition to turmeric, which gives it the deep yellow hue.

3 tablespoons ground coriander

2 tablespoons ground cumin

1 tablespoon ground turmeric

2 teaspoons ground ginger

1 teaspoon dry mustard

1 teaspoon ground green cardamom seeds

1 teaspoon freshly ground black pepper

1 teaspoon cayenne pepper

1. In a small bowl, mix the coriander, cumin, turmeric, ginger, mustard, cardamom, black pepper, and cayenne.

2. Store in an airtight container until ready to use.

TIP: To adjust the spice level of this curry blend, replace cayenne pepper with Kashmiri red chili powder for medium, or paprika for mild.

Berbere

VEGAN • VEGETARIAN • DAIRY-FREE • GLUTEN-FREE • NUT-FREE

Makes:
½ cup

Cook Time:
2 minutes

Total Time:
13 minutes

Berbere is a hot spicy blend that is integral to Ethiopian cuisine. Made with a combination of warming spices and hot chiles, this complex seasoning is used extensively in various dishes, including lentils, vegetable and meat stews, and grilled meats. This blend is made from a combination of toasted whole spices and a few preground ones.

4 teaspoons coriander seeds

2 teaspoons cumin seeds

2 teaspoons fenugreek seeds

2 teaspoons black peppercorns

2 teaspoons green cardamom seeds

10 cloves

2 teaspoons cayenne powder

6 tablespoons paprika

1 teaspoon ground ginger

1 teaspoon ground cinnamon

½ teaspoon ground nutmeg

2 teaspoons turmeric powder

2 teaspoons salt

1. Lightly toast the coriander, cumin, fenugreek, peppercorns, cardamom seeds, and cloves in a sauté pan or skillet over medium heat for 2 minutes, until fragrant. Stir often.

2. Turn off the heat and transfer to a plate to stop the cooking. Cool for 10 minutes.

3. Put the toasted spices in a spice or coffee grinder and grind to a fine powder. Next, add the cayenne, paprika, ginger, cinnamon, nutmeg, turmeric, and salt and grind briefly.

4. Transfer to an airtight container and store in a dark and cool place.

TIP: This recipe makes a medium-spicy blend. To make it mild, skip the cayenne pepper.

Harissa Paste

VEGAN • VEGETARIAN • DAIRY-FREE • GLUTEN-FREE • NUT-FREE

Serves:
About
4 ounces

Prep Time:
5 minutes

Total Time:
8 minutes

Harissa is a North African hot chile pepper paste that is traditionally served alongside bread, stews, and couscous dishes. Recipes vary widely, but it is typically made with either roasted red peppers, Baklouti peppers, or serrano peppers, along with a blend of spices, including caraway seeds, cumin seeds, coriander seeds, garlic paste, and olive oil. In this recipe, I use a combination of red pepper flakes and ancho chili powder to make a flavorful chili paste.

2 teaspoons coriander seeds

1 teaspoon cumin seeds

½ teaspoon caraway or fennel seeds

1 tablespoon paprika

1 tablespoon ancho chili powder

1 teaspoon red pepper flakes

1 teaspoon sea salt

2 tablespoons sun-dried tomatoes or 1 tablespoon tomato paste

4 garlic cloves, minced

2 tablespoons olive oil

1. Lightly toast the coriander, cumin, and caraway seeds in a sauté pan or skillet over medium heat for 2 minutes, stirring often. Transfer to a plate and cool for 5 minutes.

2. In a food processor, put in the toasted spices and the paprika, ancho chili powder, red pepper flakes, salt, tomatoes, garlic, and olive oil and blend to a smooth paste. Scrape the sides in between. Use 1 to 2 tablespoons of water if needed to blend.

TIP: Traditionally, dried red chiles are soaked in hot water for 30 minutes, then deseeded and used in this paste. To use those, skip the chili powder and red pepper flakes, and add 15 New Mexico or ancho chiles instead.

Red Curry Paste // GAENG PHET

VEGAN • VEGETARIAN • DAIRY-FREE • GLUTEN-FREE • NUT-FREE

Makes:
About
4 ounces

Prep Time:
15 minutes

Total Time:
15 minutes

Nam Prik Gaeng Phet, which means "spicy curry paste," is one of the most popular Thai curry bases. There are a few variants of red curry paste, but this one is the most commonly used. It is used in soups, curries, and as a base for condiments like the popular satay sauce. By making it at home, you can adjust the spice level to your taste.

10 dried whole red chiles

1 tablespoon coriander seeds

1 teaspoon cumin seeds

1 teaspoon whole black peppercorns

1 teaspoon salt

½ to 1 teaspoon cayenne powder

3 tablespoons lemongrass paste (see Tip)

1-inch ginger, peeled

2 teaspoons lime zest

1 tablespoon cilantro stems

2 large shallots

6 garlic cloves

2 teaspoons paprika (for color—optional)

1. Soak the dried chiles in boiling water for 10 minutes. In the meantime, in a sauté pan or skillet over medium heat, lightly toast coriander, cumin, and black peppercorns. Transfer to a plate and cool.

2. Drain the chiles, remove the seeds, and put them in a blender. Add the toasted spices, salt, cayenne, lemongrass paste, ginger, lime zest, cilantro, shallots, garlic, and paprika (if using) to the blender and grind to a smooth paste.

3. Transfer to an airtight glass jar and refrigerate until ready to use. Alternatively, freeze for up to 3 months.

Yellow Curry Paste // GAENG KAREE

VEGAN • VEGETARIAN • DAIRY-FREE • GLUTEN-FREE • NUT-FREE

Makes:
About
4 ounces

Prep Time:
15 minutes

Total Time:
15 minutes

Yellow curry paste is the mildest curry base in Thai cuisine. With coriander, cumin, and turmeric being prominent ingredients, this curry paste is a fine blend of Indian and Thai flavors. Thai yellow curry is mostly used with chicken and a starchy vegetable like potatoes. But its mild flavors make it an ideal base for seafood and tofu as well.

5 dried whole red chiles

3 tablespoons mild Curry Powder (page 151)

1 teaspoon fennel seeds

1 teaspoon salt

1 teaspoon turmeric

2 tablespoons lemongrass paste

1-inch ginger, peeled

10 garlic cloves

1 large shallot

1. Soak the dried chiles in boiling water for 10 minutes.

2. Drain the chiles, remove the seeds, and put them in a blender. Add the curry powder, fennel, salt, turmeric, lemongrass paste, ginger, garlic, and shallot to the blender and grind to a smooth paste.

3. Transfer to an airtight glass jar and refrigerate until ready to use. Alternatively, freeze for up to 3 months.

TIP: If you don't have all the ingredients for a curry powder, you can add 1 tablespoon of coriander seeds, 2 teaspoons of cumin seeds, ½ teaspoon of black peppercorns, and 1½ teaspoons of turmeric instead. Lightly toast the coriander, cumin, and peppercorns for 2 minutes over medium heat before using.

Green Curry Paste // GAENG KIEW WAN

VEGAN • VEGETARIAN • DAIRY-FREE • GLUTEN-FREE • NUT-FREE

Makes:
About
8 ounces

Prep Time:
15 minutes

Total Time:
15 minutes

Gaeng Kiew Wan means "sweet green curry" in Thai. Unlike other Thai curry pastes, which consist of dried red chiles, this blend is made with fresh green chiles, making it the spiciest of all Thai pastes. Some variations reduce the proportion of green chiles and add cilantro stems and basil leaves instead to achieve its signature green color, while controlling the spice level. This is my version of a bright, spicy, and unique curry paste.

1 tablespoon coriander seeds

1 teaspoon cumin seeds

1 teaspoon whole white peppercorns, or 1 teaspoon ground white pepper

10 Thai green bird's-eye chiles (or 3 to 4 serrano chiles), seeded and stemmed

2 jalapeño peppers, seeded and stemmed

1 teaspoon salt

3 tablespoons lemongrass paste

2 inches ginger, peeled or 1 inch galangal

1 teaspoon kaffir or regular lime zest

2 tablespoons cilantro stems

¼ cup Thai basil leaves

2 large shallots

6 garlic cloves

1. Lightly toast coriander, cumin, and peppercorns for 2 minutes in a sauté pan or skillet over medium heat. Transfer to a plate and cool.

2. In a blender, put the toasted spices, Thai chiles, peppers, salt, lemongrass paste, ginger, kaffir, cilantro, Thai basil, shallots, and garlic and blend to a smooth paste.

3. Transfer to an airtight glass jar and refrigerate until ready to use. Alternatively, freeze for up to 3 months.

Basmati Rice (White and Brown)

VEGAN • VEGETARIAN • DAIRY-FREE • GLUTEN-FREE • NUT-FREE

Serves:
3

Prep Time:
10 minutes

Cook Time:
White Rice:
6 minutes;
Brown Rice:
22 minutes on
high pressure

Release:
Natural
release for
5 minutes,
followed by
quick

Total Time:
White Rice:
31 minutes;
Brown Rice:
38 minutes

Basmati rice is an aromatic long-grained variety with a slight nutty flavor. It is grown in the northern regions of India and Pakistan. Deriving its name from the Sanskrit word "basmati," which means "fragrant," it is known for its fluffy and separated grains and is a staple with curries across the Indian subcontinent.

1 cup basmati rice

1¼ cups water

1 teaspoon canola oil or ghee

½ teaspoon salt

1. Soak the rice for 10 minutes (white rice only). Rinse 2 or 3 times until water runs clear.

2. Put the drained rice, water, oil, and salt in the cooking insert and stir.

3. Lock the lid in place. Select manual or pressure cook and adjust to high. Cook for 6 minutes for white rice, or 22 minutes for brown rice, on sealing mode.

4. When the cooking is complete, let the pressure release naturally for 5 minutes, followed by a quick pressure release as per your cooker instructions. Unlock and remove the lid.

5. Using a fork, gently fluff the rice, and enjoy!

TIP: Soaking is key to getting a fluffy texture for white rice. It gets rid of excess starch and results in each grain being separated. It is not required for brown basmati rice because it doesn't have the starch coating.

Jasmine Rice (White and Brown)

VEGAN • VEGETARIAN • DAIRY-FREE • GLUTEN-FREE • NUT-FREE

Serves:
3

Prep Time:
1 minute

Cook Time:
White rice:
6 minutes on
high pressure;
brown rice:
22 minutes on
high pressure

Release:
Natural
release for
5 minutes,
followed by
quick

Total Time:
White rice:
22 minutes;
brown tice:
38 minutes

Jasmine rice is a long-grain rice variety native to Thailand, commonly used in Southeast Asian cuisine. The grains are shorter and thicker than basmati rice and have a slightly sticky texture when cooked. Jasmine rice is known for a delicate floral aroma and slightly sweet taste.

1 cup Jasmine rice

1¼ cups water

1 teaspoon canola or coconut oil

½ teaspoon salt

1. Rinse the rice 2 or 3 times until water runs clear.

2. Put the drained rice, water, oil, and salt in the cooking insert and stir.

3. Lock the lid in place. Select manual or pressure cook and adjust to high. Cook for 6 minutes for white rice, or 22 minutes for brown rice, on sealing mode.

4. When the cooking is complete, let the pressure release naturally for 5 minutes, followed by a quick pressure release as per your cooker's instructions. Unlock and remove the lid.

5. Using a fork, gently fluff the rice, and enjoy!

TIP: If you're never tried Jasmine rice before, the texture is stickier than Basmati or most American long-grain varieties of rice. Rinsing the rice before cooking washes off the excess starch, which results in the ideal texture.

Coconut Rice

VEGAN • VEGETARIAN • DAIRY-FREE • GLUTEN-FREE

Serves:
3

Prep Time:
1 minute

Cook Time:
6 minutes on
high pressure

Release:
Natural
release for
5 minutes,
followed by
quick

Total Time:
22 minutes

Fragrant Jasmine rice cooked with creamy, rich coconut milk is the perfect side dish for most Thai and some Asian curries. The naturally sweet coconut milk complements the aromatic Jasmine rice really well. It is such a simple way to elevate an everyday side dish.

1 cup Jasmine rice, rinsed well
¾ cup coconut milk

½ cup water
¼ teaspoon salt

1. Rinse rice 2 or 3 times until water runs clear.

2. Put the drained rice, coconut milk, water, and salt in the cooking insert and stir.

3. Lock the lid in place. Select manual or pressure cook and adjust to high. Cook for 6 minutes on sealing mode.

4. When the cooking is complete, let the pressure release naturally for 5 minutes, followed by a quick pressure release as per your cooker instructions. Unlock and remove the lid.

5. Using a fork, gently fluff the rice, and enjoy!

TIP: Full-fat coconut milk gives the best results in this recipe. After cooking, you may see specks of coconut milk fat on top of the rice. Gently toss the rice with a fork to mix it in.

Cumin Rice // JEERA PULAO

VEGETARIAN • DAIRY-FREE • GLUTEN-FREE

Serves:
3

Prep Time:
10 minutes

Cook Time:
7 minutes
(1 minute on sauté,
6 minutes on
high pressure)

Release:
Natural release for
5 minutes,
followed by
quick

Total Time:
32 minutes

Soft, fluffy grains of basmati rice flavored with an earthy, sweet flavor is the perfect accompaniment for most North Indian and Pakistani curries. Cumin is called Jeera in Hindi, a local North Indian language. In this recipe, cumin seeds are lightly toasted in ghee along with cardamom and bay leaf to release their aroma and flavor into the water. When the rice is cooked in this flavored liquid, it absorbs the nutty flavor of cumin.

1 teaspoon ghee or canola oil

1 teaspoon cumin seeds

2 to 3 green cardamom pods

1 bay leaf

1 cup basmati rice

1¼ cups water

½ teaspoon salt

1. Preheat the electric pressure cooker by selecting sauté. When the inner pot is hot, after about 30 seconds, put in the ghee, cumin seeds, cardamom pods, and bay leaf.

2. When the cumin begins to sizzle, add the rice, water, and salt. Give it a stir and turn off sauté.

3. Lock the lid in place. Select manual or pressure cook and adjust to high. Cook for 6 minutes on sealing mode.

4. When the cooking is complete, let the pressure release naturally for 5 minutes, followed by a quick pressure release as per your cooker instructions. Unlock and remove the lid.

5. Using a fork, gently fluff the rice, and enjoy!

TIP: Add ½ cup of frozen peas into the rice and enjoy a popular variation called Peas Pulao.

Spanish Rice // ARROZ ROJO

VEGAN • VEGETARIAN • DAIRY-FREE • GLUTEN-FREE • NUT-FREE

Serves:
3

Prep Time:
5 minutes

Cook Time:
11 minutes
(5 minutes on
sauté,
6 minutes on
high pressure)

Release:
Natural
release for
5 minutes,
followed by
quick

Total Time:
31 minutes

Spanish rice is a Mexican side dish made by sautéing white rice in oil until it turns golden brown in color. Tomatoes, garlic, and onions are added and then the rice is cooked until it is fluffy. Also known as Mexican Rice, Arroz Rojo, or simply Red Rice, it is known for its simple flavors and orange-red hue. This delicious side is commonly served with meat stews, beans, and grilled entrées.

1 tablespoon olive oil

1 cup long-grain white rice, rinsed 2 or 3 times

½ onion, finely chopped

1 garlic clove, minced

1 tablespoon tomato paste

½ teaspoon dried oregano

½ teaspoon ground cumin

½ teaspoon salt

1¼ cups water

2 tablespoons cilantro (for garnish)

1. Preheat the electric pressure cooker by selecting sauté. When the inner pot is hot, after about 30 seconds, put in the oil and rinsed rice. Toast the rice for 4 to 5 minutes, stirring a few times.

2. Add the onion and garlic, and sauté for another minute. Add the tomato paste, oregano, cumin, salt, and water and stir. Turn off sauté.

3. Lock the lid in place. Select manual or pressure cook and adjust to high. Cook for 6 minutes on sealing mode.

4. When the cooking is complete, let the pressure release naturally for 5 minutes, followed by a quick pressure release as per your cooker instructions. Unlock and remove the lid.

5. Using a fork, gently fluff the rice, and garnish with cilantro!

Roti // CHAPATI

VEGETARIAN • DAIRY-FREE • NUT-FREE

Makes:
12 roti

Prep Time:
5 minutes
plus
15 minutes for
resting

Total Time:
38 minutes

Roti, also known as chapati or phulka, are flatbreads made with whole wheat flour. They are a staple in most Indian homes and are typically served as a side with curries. The dough for roti is made with flour and water and is ready for use without any fermentation.

2 cups whole wheat flour, plus ¼ cup, divided

¾ to 1 cup water, or as needed, divided

2 teaspoons olive oil

1. In a large mixing bowl, pour 2 cups flour and ¼ cup of water. Using your fingers, gently mix the dough until all the water is absorbed.

2. Add another ¼ cup water and keep mixing until it starts to form the dough. Depending on the brand of your flour, you will need ¾ to 1 cup of water. In the end, the dough should be soft but not sticky.

3. Using your fist or lower palm, knead the dough for 1 minute. Lift the furthest edge of the dough and repeatedly fold it back over toward you. Wet your hand to smooth the dough. Add the oil and knead for another 30 seconds.

4. Cover it with a damp kitchen towel and rest for 15 minutes for the glutens to develop. After that, knead the dough once again.

5. To make the roti, divide the dough into 12 equal portions about the size of a golf ball and roll in your palms to make a round ball. Cover all dough balls with a damp towel.

6. Put the other ¼ cup flour on a plate for dusting the dough while rolling. Ensure that your rolling pin and surface is dry.

7. Take one dough ball at a time, keeping the remaining dough covered with a damp towel so they don't dry out.

8. Dip the dough ball in the plate of dry flour, shake off the excess, then put it on the rolling surface and flatten it gently using your hand.

9. Start rolling gently from the center in an outward motion, turning it about 45 degrees between each roll. Dust with flour in between to prevent sticking.

10. Continue rolling until you flatten the dough into an even disc about 7 inches in diameter.

11. Preheat a nonstick sauté pan or skillet over medium-high heat.

12. Dust off the excess flour from the rolled roti and place flat in the skillet. Cook the roti until small bumps start forming on the surface. Depending on how hot your skillet is, it can be anywhere between 30 to 45 seconds. Using tongs, flip the roti.

13. Cook until you see bumps develop on this side, about 15 to 20 seconds, then flip.

14. Using a flat spatula, gently press the roti while rotating it, until it begins to puff up.

15. Flip it a few times to cook it evenly. Remove it and place onto a paper-towel-lined plate or tortilla case. Repeat the process for other roti. Enjoy warm with your favorite curry.

TIP: To enhance the flavor of roti, brush them with butter or ghee right after they finish cooking. That also keeps them moist and soft longer.

Buttered Couscous

VEGETARIAN • NUT-FREE

Serves:
3

Prep Time:
1 minute

Cook Time:
2 minutes on
high pressure

Release:
Natural

Total Time:
20 minutes

Couscous is a type of small pasta made of steamed durum wheat semolina. This national dish of Morocco has been a staple in North Africa for centuries and is traditionally served as a base to soak up curries and stews. You can enjoy it plain, like in this recipe, or add pine nuts, dried fruit, and chopped herbs to make a fancier variation of this popular side.

1 tablespoon unsalted butter	½ teaspoon salt
1 cup couscous (fine)	1¾ cups water

1. Put the butter, couscous, salt, and water in the cooking insert and give it a stir.

2. Lock the lid in place. Select manual or pressure cook and adjust to high. Cook for 2 minutes on sealing mode.

3. When the cooking is complete, let the pressure release naturally; it should take around 5 to 7 minutes. Unlock and remove the lid.

4. Using a fork, gently fluff the couscous, and enjoy!

TIP: To enhance the flavor of couscous, use chicken stock instead of water and add a ½ teaspoon of Italian seasoning.

ELECTRIC PRESSURE COOKER TIME CHARTS

The following charts provide approximate cook times used for a variety of foods in a 6-quart electric pressure cooker like the Instant Pot. Larger electric pressure cookers may need a little extra time to cook. To begin, you may want to cook for a minute or two less than the times listed; you can always simmer foods at natural pressure to finish cooking.

Keep in mind that these times apply to the foods when partially submerged in water (or broth), steamed, or cooked alone. However, the cooking times for a given food may differ when it's used in different recipes, because of additional ingredients or cooking liquids, a different release method than the one listed here, and so on.

For any foods labeled "natural release," allow at least 15 minutes of natural pressure release before quick releasing any remaining pressure.

BEANS AND LEGUMES

When cooking a pound or more of beans, it's best to use low pressure and increase the cooking time by a minute or two, because larger amounts at high pressure are prone to foaming. If you have less than a pound of beans, high pressure is fine. A little oil in the cooking liquid will reduce foaming as well.

Unless a shorter release time is indicated, let the pressure release naturally for at least 15 minutes, after which any remaining pressure can be quick released.

	Minutes under Pressure Unsoaked	Minutes under Pressure Soaked in Salted water	Pressure	Release
Black beans	22 25	10 12	High Low	Natural
Black-eyed peas	12 15	5 7	High Low	Natural for 8 minutes, then quick
Cannellini beans	25 28	8 10	High Low	Natural
Chickpeas (garbanzo beans)	18 20	3 4	High Low	Natural for 3 minutes, then quick
Kidney beans	25 28	8 10	High Low	Natural
Lentils	10	Not recommended	High	Quick
Lima beans	15 18	4 5	High Low	Natural for 5 minutes, then quick
Navy beans	18 20	8 10	High Low	Natural
Pinto beans	25 28	10 12	High Low	Natural
Soybeans, dried	25 28	12 14	High Low	Natural
Soybeans, fresh (edamame)	1	Not recommended	High	Quick
Split peas (unsoaked)	5 (firm peas) to 8 (soft peas)	Not recommended	High	Natural

MEAT

Except as noted, the times below are for braised meats—that is, meats that are seared before pressure cooking and partially submerged in liquid. Unless a shorter release time is indicated, let the pressure release naturally for at least 15 minutes, after which any remaining pressure can be quick released.

	Minutes under Pressure	Pressure	Release
Beef, shoulder (chuck), 2" chunks	20	High	Natural for 10 minutes
Beef, shoulder (chuck) roast (2 lb.)	35	High	Natural
Beef, bone-in short ribs	40	High	Natural
Beef, flat iron steak, cut into ½" strips	1	Low	Quick
Beef, sirloin steak, cut into ½" strips	1	Low	Quick
Lamb, shanks	40	High	Natural
Lamb, shoulder, 2" chunks	35	High	Natural
Pork, back ribs (steamed)	30	High	Quick
Pork, shoulder, 2" chunks	20	High	Natural
Pork, shoulder roast (2 lb.)	25	High	Natural
Pork, smoked sausage, ½" slices	20	High	Quick
Pork, spare ribs (steamed)	20	High	Quick
Pork, tenderloin	4	Low	Quick

POULTRY

Except as noted, the times below are for poultry that is partially submerged in liquid. Unless a shorter release time is indicated, let the pressure release naturally for at least 15 minutes, after which any remaining pressure can be quick released.

	Minutes under Pressure	Pressure	Release
Chicken breast, bone-in (steamed)	8	Low	Natural for 5 minutes
Chicken breast, boneless (steamed)	5	Low	Natural for 8 minutes
Chicken thigh, bone-in	15	High	Natural for 10 minutes
Chicken thigh, boneless	8	High	Natural for 10 minutes
Chicken thigh, boneless, 1"–2" pieces	5	High	Quick
Chicken, whole (seared on all sides)	12–14	Low	Natural for 8 minutes
Duck quarters, bone-in	35	High	Quick
Turkey breast, tenderloin (12 oz.) (steamed)	5	Low	Natural for 8 minutes
Turkey thigh, bone-in	30	High	Natural

SEAFOOD

All times are for steamed fish and shellfish.

	Minutes under Pressure	Pressure	Release
Clams	2	High	Quick
Halibut, fresh (1" thick)	3	High	Quick
Large shrimp, frozen	1	Low	Quick
Mussels	1	High	Quick
Salmon, fresh (1" thick)	5	Low	Quick
Tilapia or cod, fresh	1	Low	Quick
Tilapia or cod, frozen	3	Low	Quick

MEASUREMENT CONVERSIONS

VOLUME EQUIVALENTS (LIQUID)

US Standard	US Standard (ounces)	Metric (approximate)
2 tablespoons	1 fl. oz.	30 mL
¼ cup	2 fl. oz.	60 mL
½ cup	4 fl. oz.	120 mL
1 cup	8 fl. oz.	240 mL
1½ cups	12 fl. oz.	355 mL
2 cups or 1 pint	16 fl. oz.	475 mL
4 cups or 1 quart	32 fl. oz.	1 L
1 gallon	128 fl. oz.	4 L

OVEN TEMPERATURES

Fahrenheit (F)	Celsius (C) (approximate)
250°F	120°C
300°F	150°C
325°F	165°C
350°F	180°C
375°F	190°C
400°F	200°C
425°F	220°C
450°F	230°C

VOLUME EQUIVALENTS (DRY)

US Standard	Metric (approximate)
⅛ teaspoon	0.5 mL
¼ teaspoon	1 mL
½ teaspoon	2 mL
¾ teaspoon	4 mL
1 teaspoon	5 mL
1 tablespoon	15 mL
¼ cup	59 mL
⅓ cup	79 mL
½ cup	118 mL
⅔ cup	156 mL
¾ cup	177 mL
1 cup	235 mL
2 cups or 1 pint	475 mL
3 cups	700 mL
4 cups or 1 quart	1 L

WEIGHT EQUIVALENTS

US Standard	Metric (approximate)
½ ounce	15 g
1 ounce	30 g
2 ounces	60 g
4 ounces	115 g
8 ounces	225 g
12 ounces	340 g
16 ounces or 1 pound	455 g

INGREDIENT GLOSSARY

adobo seasoning: A Mexican base seasoning used to flavor curries and stews. This spice mix is made of garlic powder, onion powder, oregano, paprika, chili powder, salt, and pepper.

adobo sauce: A traditional earthy and tangy Mexican sauce made with local chilies, like ancho and guajillo, garlic, cumin, cinnamon, oregano, salt, and vinegar.

amchur: Also referred to as amchoor, this tangy spice powder is made from dried green mangoes and is used to add tart flavors to Indian curries.

berbere: An Ethiopian spice blend very similar to the Indian Garam Masala (page 150), berbere is used to provide heat and a red hue to curries.

chaat masala: A tangy seasoning blend used in the Indian subcontinent. It is used to add a zing to salads, curries, fruits, snacks, drinks, and more.

coconut cream: Coconut cream is the thick, nonliquid part that separates and rises to the top of the coconut milk can. To get that, open a can without shaking it and skim off the top cream part with a spoon.

coriander: The pale green seeds of the cilantro plant used to make spice powders or blends for curries around the world.

cumin: The aromatic seeds used whole or ground to add an earthy, sweet flavor to the dish.

curry leaves: Leaves of a plant, used extensively in South Indian cooking for adding a zesty aroma and flavor.

curry powder: A mild alternative of the Indian Garam Masala (page 150), created by the British in the 1800s. This spice mix is used in many global cuisines and consists of coriander, cumin, and turmeric along with other fragrant spices.

dried fenugreek leaves: Also known as kasoori methi. These sun-dried leaves of the fenugreek plant are often added as a finishing ingredient in rich Indian curries and sauces.

galangal: Also known as Thai ginger, galangal is used in making Thai curry pastes and has a woody, sharp, and citrusy flavor.

garam masala: Indian spice blend made of toasted coriander, cumin, cardamom, cloves, peppercorns, cinnamon, and bay leaves. Some variations may also include fennel, nutmeg and black cardamom.

ghee: A form of clarified butter in which milk solids separate leaving behind a clear fat. It is used extensively in Indian cooking.

Greek yogurt: A thick yogurt that has been strained to remove most of the whey. Its thicker consistency is ideal for marinades and for thickening curries.

harissa: A North African hot chile pepper paste that is traditionally served alongside bread, stews, and couscous dishes.

heeng: Also called asafetida and hing, this spice is often added to lentil and bean curries in Indian cuisine.

kaffir lime leaves: The leaves of a native Thai citrus fruit variety called kaffir lime are used extensively in South Asian dishes. Look for them in the refrigerated produce aisle of Asian stores. Lime zest acts as a close substitute. For 4 to 6 lime leaves, add 1 teaspoon lime zest instead.

Kashmiri red chili powder: Local chiles native to Kashmir in Northern India. Available whole or in ground form from Indian stores, international food markets, or online, these are used for adding a vibrant red hue and mild heat to a dish. A close substitute for this ground spice is a combination of paprika and cayenne. 1 teaspoon Kashmiri red chili powder = 1 teaspoon paprika + ¼ teaspoon cayenne powder

lemongrass: This is a Thai herb that provides a lemony aroma and flavor to many Southeast Asian dishes. You can find it fresh in the produce aisle or in a paste form in the refrigerated produce section of your supermarket.

palak: Hindi name for spinach. Commonly used in a popular North Indian curry called Palak Paneer (page 48). It is often confused for the term "saag," which refers to a combination of dark greens.

paneer: A firm Indian cottage cheese made by curdling milk with lime juice, paneer is a great source of protein in Indian vegetarian dishes.

ras el hanout: An aromatic spice blend used extensively in Moroccan cooking.

sazon: An aromatic brightly colored spice blend used extensively in Latin American cooking for adding color and flavor.

sofrito: Also known as *soffritto*, this aromatic sauce is used as a base for many curries and stews in Latin American and Spanish cuisine. It is made by pureeing together onion, garlic, bell peppers, and cilantro. Some variations also include tomato.

RESOURCES

Online support communities for electric pressure cookers on Facebook are a great resource for recipes, tips and general questions. These include popular Facebook groups like:

- Instant Pot Community
- Instant Pot Recipes Only
- Instant Pot for Beginners
- Mealthy Pressure Cooker Community.

INDEX

ACKNOWLEDGMENTS

O n January 2, 2020, my husband asked me, "What are your top five goals for this year?" The first thing I said was: "I want to write a cookbook!" Little did I know that the universe would align and set me on the path to accomplishing this goal so soon. For that, I am really grateful!

I believe that behind every woman who sets out to achieve success, there is a village that supports her. My tiny village is filled with the following people who have contributed to my life and this book in their own special ways. I have each one to thank for being a part of my journey.

My parents, who always believed in me more than I did. My dad taught me that it's never too late to pursue your dreams, and I inherited his passion to experiment with flavors. Papa, you would have been so proud of this book. Miss you! My mom taught me that you don't have to spend hours in the kitchen to cook healthy and tasty meals. Thank you for giving me a solid foundation.

My husband, my rock! Thank you for always encouraging me to reach for the stars and being my sous chef and recipe taster and for critiquing my creations in the most honest (and daring) way. Thanks, also, for cleaning up the tornado of a mess that I left behind after recipe testing. Most important, thank you for catching me whenever I fall.

My girls, my life! I started my recipe website to teach you two how to cook. Some of the best memories in my life are of cooking and baking with you. Thank you for supporting me throughout the making of this book, making schedules for me, then checking on my progress. I'm sure you had fun "mommying" me around. Thank you for being my guinea pigs, for eating the same recipe, sometimes meal after meal, until I perfected it, and still appreciating it as if you were tasting it for the first time. Motherhood made me really evolve as a cook, and I have you both to thank for it.

A heartfelt thanks to my foodie girlfriends for helping me test some of these recipes and perfect them.

My readers, I cannot thank you enough for all the support you have shown me over the past few years. Thank you for trying my recipes, sharing them, and making my day by leaving thoughtful messages on my blog. I could not have come this far without you.

And last but not least, thank you to the entire Callisto Media team, for giving me this opportunity and helping me accomplish my goal. Special thanks to my editor, Gurvinder, for your valuable feedback and support.

ABOUT THE AUTHOR

Aneesha Gupta is a recipe developer, photographer, writer, and food blogger. She is the founder of Spice Cravings (spicecravings.com), where she shares quick and easy international recipes that are low in effort and big on taste. With step-by-step instructions and smart short-cuts, these recipes are easy and doable for busy families, even on weeknights.

She started cooking as a teen by helping her mother, and she quickly developed a passion for food and cooking. Aneesha's recipes are inspired by her North Indian Punjabi roots, world travels (18 countries and counting), and life as a working mother. Her work has been featured on NBC News, Yahoo, MSN, Instant Pot, Delish, and more.

Aneesha lives in the San Francisco Bay Area with her husband and twin daughters. When she's not working or playing mommy, you'll find her cooking with her family or watching romantic comedies and reruns of *Friends* or *The Office* with a cup of coffee or a glass of wine.

For any feedback or questions, you can reach her at aneesha@spice-cravings.com, or via her social media channels:

Facebook: facebook.com/spicecravings

Instagram: instagram.com/spicecravings

Pinterest: pinterest.com/spicecravings

Printed in the USA
CPSIA information can be obtained
at www.ICGtesting.com
CBHW040738280124
3678CB00002B/15